For the woollies!

Ivan Doig

HEART EARTH

HEART EARTH

IVAN DOIG

ATHENEUM   NEW YORK   1993

Maxwell Macmillan Canada
Toronto

Maxwell Macmillan International
New York   Oxford   Singapore   Sydney

Copyright © 1993 by Ivan Doig

All rights reserved. No part of this book may be reproduced or transmitted in any form or by any means, electronic or mechanical, including photocopying, recording, or by any information storage and retrieval system, without permission in writing from the Publisher.

Atheneum
Macmillan Publishing Company
866 Third Avenue
New York, NY 10022

Maxwell Macmillan Canada, Inc.
1200 Eglinton Avenue East
Suite 200
Don Mills, Ontario M3C 3N1

Macmillan Publishing Company is part of the Maxwell
Communication Group of Companies.

Library of Congress Cataloging-in-Publication Data
Doig, Ivan.
Heart earth / by Ivan Doig.
p.   cm.
ISBN 0-689-12137-7
1. Doig, Ivan—Family.   2. Novelists, American—20th century—
Biography—Family.   3. Novelists, American—Montana—Biography—
Family.   4. Ranch life—Montana.   5. Montana—Biography.   I. Title.
PS3554.O415Z468   1993   92-46904   CIP
813'.54—dc20
[B]

Macmillan books are available at special discounts for bulk
purchases for sales promotions, premiums, fund-raising,
or educational use. For details, contact:

Special Sales Director
Macmillan Publishing Company
866 Third Avenue
New York, NY 10022

Book Design by Anne Scatto

10 9 8 7 6 5 4 3 2 1

Printed in the United States of America

For
Carol Doig
Linda Bierds
and
Sydney Kaplan
when we traveled the Montana heart and perimeter,
and won at electronic poker, too

AUTHOR'S NOTE

The chain lightning of memory and family never quits in us. Fifteen years ago, I made a book out of the pair of reliably stormy antagonists—Charlie Doig, my father, and my mother's mother, Bessie Ringer—who bent their lives to give me mine:

"Here is a man and here a woman. In the coming light of one June morning, the same piece of life is axed away from each of them. Wounded hard, they go off to their private ways. Until at last the wifeless man offers across to the daughter-robbed woman. And I am the agreed barter between them."

This House of Sky set out the story of how, after the loss of my mother in 1945, those stricken two—we three—struggled ourselves into becoming a family and staying one. Told and done, I thought with satisfaction, as that book took on a life of its own with 150,000 readers. Until a day when my mother's letters from that end-of-war year found their way to me. Their record of ricochet was stunning: from American deserts and mountaintops to a ship in combat in the South Pacific to a family trunk closed away for forty-one years to a last will and testament to, at very last, a son's eyes. Line by line Berneta Ringer Doig's own report, from the turbulent half-year before the opening pages of *This House of Sky*, could go from commonplace to searing, from sassy gossip to monumental anguish.

Out of that unexpected narrative of hers comes this saga-within-a-family-saga, of an indelible young woman and the resonances of heart and earth.

Intervals of dreaming help us to
stand up under days of work.

—Pablo Neruda, *Memoirs*

HEART EARTH

PHOENIX
FEB 5
9 PM
1945
ARIZ.
2

Dear Wally—

. . . I shouldn't even be writing you my troubles but I have to spill over to someone. I'd just like to have you around so I could put my head on your shoulder and cry.

. . . It is going on 1 and we haven't had dinner yet. Charlie is resting and I thought the rest would do him more good than eating. Ivan is out in the backyard building roads. He had a fox-hole dug you could bury a cow in.

In that last winter of the war, she knew to use pointblank ink. Nothing is ever crossed out, never a p.s., the heart-quick lines still as distinct as the day of the postmark, her fountain pen instinctively refusing the fade of time. Among the little I have had of her is that pen. Incised into the demure barrel of it—my father must have birth-dayed her a couple of weeks' worth of his cowhand wages in this gesture—rests her maiden name. Readily enough, then, I can make out the hand at the page, the swift skritch of her letters racing down onto paper for Wally—someone—to know. But all else of her, this woman there earmarking a warstriped airmail envelope with the return address of *Mrs. Chas. Doig*, has been only farthest childscapes, half-rememberings thinned by so many years since. I had given up ever trying to uncurtain my mother. Now her pages begin her: *I have to spill over* . . . Upward from her held pen, at last she is back again.

Aluminum and Arizona in their wartime tryst produced Alzona Park, the defense workers' housing project which had been feeling my shovel ever since my parents and I alit there. I knew, with the full mania of a five-year-old, that the project's barren back yards necessitated my toy-truck roads for strafing, bombing—World War Two had a lot of destruction to be played at yet. I was lonesome for my foxhole, though. By a turn of events you couldn't foresee in desert warfare it had been put out of service by rain, my mother making me fill the dirt back into the brimming crater lest somebody underestimate it as a puddle and go in up to the neck.

Spies, saboteurs, the kind of subversive traffic you get in back yards seemed to me to deserve precisely such a ducking, but my mother stood firm on foxholelessness. I suppose she had in mind our standing with our Alzonan barracks neighbors, who, if she would just trust my reports, all the more justified a foxhole: hunker in there, peeking over the earthrim, and see what they turned into, housewife snipers in the 200 building to be fended off with a pretend rifle, *pchoo pchoo*, the long 300 building a sudden Japanese battleship, the foxhole now needing to be a gun battery on the destroyer USS *Ault*, blazing away at those fiends threatening our aircraft carriers, holding them at bay until down in the torpedo room Wally—

Wally. February 17, 1986. Four fingers of flame thrust toward the snowfields of Mount Baldy and extinguish into echo. Stiffly working their rifle bolts to reload, the Veterans of Foreign Wars honor guard aims and lets fire again, the combined muzzleflash flexing bright another instant. Then a last volley, and the honor guard dissolves into World War Two oldsters clutching at their campaign caps in the cemetery wind.

Ceremonially Wally Ringer's chapter of life was over, that wind-ridden afternoon. But in the family plot of time, not nearly done with. Can this be what that brother of my mother had in mind with the letters, sensing the carrying power of ink as a way to go on? By making me heir to the lost side of my past, to my mother's own communiqués of time and place doing to her what they did, he would find a kind of lastingness too?

At the moment I only knew I was the most grudging of pallbearers, gritting against the shiver, more than windborne, of having come back where I'd promised myself not to. To where all the compartments of my earliest self rode together on me, nephew, son, grandson, native of this valley, economic refugee from it, ranch kid, town nomad, only child awash in family attention, indrawn half-orphan. Chambered as a goddamn nautilus. Three times before, I watched a saga of my family echo into the earth here, and in the glide of years since convinced myself I was safely done with Montana burials. Those earliest voices of the heart held no more to tell, I'd thought. Wally's in particular I no longer gave ear to, even though for most of my life—most of his, as we were only fifteen years apart in age—he was that perfect conspirator, a favorite uncle. That extracurricular relative we need, some close-but-not-immediate livewire in whom the family blood always hums, never drones. As pushful through life as the canyon snowplow he piloted over black ice, bull-chested, supremely bald, with the inveterate overbite grin of my mother's people which brought the top teeth happily out on parade with the rest of him: as he'd have said it himself, quite the Wally. Here at his funeral were his first and third wives, both in utmost tears, and his second wife sent bereaved regrets from New Mexico.

In my own remembering he bursts home with that whopping grin on him, ever ready to fetch the boy me off to a trouty creek or up into the grass parks of the

Castle Mountains to sight deer or elk, or to an away game of football or basketball, never failing to sing out his announcement of our arrival, "Here we are, entertain us!" If I could but choose, the go-anywhere-but-*go* streak in this likable uncle of mine I would hold in mind, together with my go-along soberside capacity to take everything in. Avid as the Montana seasons, the team we made.

But that all went, in our weedy argument over the expenses of a funeral, no less. By the time of the death of his mother, my grandmother, in 1974, Wally and I were the only ones in what was left of the family who could take on the burial costs. Easy to misstep when trying to shoulder a debt in tandem, and we faithfully fell flat. What got into me, to ignore the first law of relatives—Thou shalt not tangle family and money—and agree that I'd temporarily stand his half of the burial bill as well as my own? What got into Wally, to succumb to the snazzier fishing pole and high-powered new hunting scope he soon was showing off to me while letting the funeral reimbursement grow tardy and tardier? In the end he never quite forgave the insult of being asked to pony up, just as I never quite forgave the insult of having to ask. (At last it occurs to me, no longer the overproud struggling young freelance writer I was then: fishpole and riflescope were Wally's own tools of eloquence, weren't they.) I left from Wallace Ringer's graveside half-ashamed of myself that I had not been able to forget our rift, the other half at him for shirking that funeral deal; the sum of it a bone anger in me that we had ended up somewhere between quibble and quarrel forever, this quicksilver uncle and I.

With the packet of letters, then, each dutifully folded back into its envelope edged with World War Two airmail emblazonments, Wally reached out past what had come between us when he was alive.

Long before, when I began to relive on paper my family's saga of trying to right ourselves after the hole that was knocked in us that year of 1945, I asked around for old letters, photos, anything, but Wally offered nothing. *This House of Sky* grew to be a book faceted with the three of us I had memory record of, my father, my grandmother, myself. Now, in the lee of my estranged uncle's funeral, his bequest. The only correspondence by my mother I'd ever seen, postmarks as direct as a line of black-on-white stepping stones toward that mid-1945 void.

I believe I know the change of heart in Wally. More than once as my writing of books went on, I would be back in Montana en route to lore or lingo along some weatherbeaten stretch of road, near Roundup or Ovando or somewhere equally far from his Deep Creek Canyon highway district, and ahead would materialize my uncle's unmistakable profile, two-thirds of him above his belt buckle, flagging me to a stop. The Montana highway department's annual desperate effort to catch up with maintenance, this was, with section men such as Wally temporarily assigned into hard hat and firebright safety vest to hold up traffic while heavy equipment labored on a piece of road. Betterments, such midsummer flurries of repairs were called. So, as wind kept trying to swat his stop sign out of his grasp, my mother's brother and I would manage to kill time with car-window conversation, Wally gingerly asking how things were in Seattle, how my writing was going, my stiff reciprocal questions about his latest fishing luck, his hunting plans for that autumn. Old bandits gone civil. When dumptrucks and graders at last paused, he would declare, "Okay, she's a go" and flag me on through to the fresh-fixed patch of blacktop. And I can only believe this was how the dying Wally saw his mending action of willing the letters to me, a betterment.

But before any of this, before the gnarl in our family history that brought me back and back to that wintry cemetery, he was a sailor on the *Ault*.

I am feeling pretty good, much better than anytime so far since I've been down here. Charlie is the one that isn't well.

A few of the letters in the packet duffeled home from the Pacific are blurry from water stains, but this first one by my mother to her sailor brother makes all too clear that we have traded predicament in Montana for predicament in Arizona.

My parents and my father's sister Anna and her husband Joe and the five-year-old dirtmover that was me had thrown what we had into a Ford coupe and pinballed our way down through the West a thousand and fifty miles, ration books straining from gas station to gas station along U.S. 89, me most of the time intrepidly shelved crosswise in the coupe's rear window, until we rolled to a halt in Phoenix the night before Thanksgiving of 1944. The next Monday my father and Joe latched on as Aluminum Company of America factory hands and our great sunward swerve settled into Alzona Park orbit.

Unit 119B, where the five of us crammed in, consisted

of a few cubicles of brown composition board, bare floors and windows howlingly curtainless until my mother could stand it no longer and hung some dimestore chintz; along with fifty-five hundred other Alzonans, we were war-loyally putting up with packing crate living conditions. But pulling in money hand over fist: my father and Joe drawing fat hourly wages at the aluminum plant—*hourly*, for guys who counted themselves lucky to make any money by the month in Montana ranchwork. Surely this, the state of Arizona humming and buzzing with defense plants and military bases installed for the war, this must be the craved new world, the shores of Social Security and the sugar trees of overtime. True, the product of defense work wasn't as indubitable as a sheep or cow. Aluminum screeched through the cutting area where Dad and Joe worked and a half-mile of factory later was shunted out as bomber wings, but all in between was secret. For the 119B batch of us to try to figure out the alchemy, my father smuggled out down his pant leg a whatzit from the wing plant. I remember the thing as about the size of the business end of a branding iron, the approximate shape of a flying V, pale as ice and almost weightless, so light to hold it was a little spooky. "I'll bet ye can't tell me what this is," Dad challenged as he plunked down the contraband piece of metal to wow my mother and Anna and me and for that matter his brother-in-law Joe. Actually he had no more idea than any of the rest of us what the mystifying gizmo was, but it must have done something supportive in the wing of a bombing plane.

Like light, time is both particle and wave. Even as that far winter of our lives traced itself as a single Arizona

amplitude of season along the collective dateline of memory, simultaneously it was stippling all through us in
instants distinct as the burn of sparks. The sunshiny
morning when suddenly the storm of hammering breaks
out and does not quit for forty days, as a hundred more
units of Alzona Park are flung up. The time Anna tries
to coax me into a trip to the project's store for an ice
cream cone and, ice cream passion notwithstanding, I will
not budge from my mother, some eddy of apprehension
holding me to where I can see her, not lose her from my
eyes even a moment. The night of downtown Phoenix
after my father and mother have splurged on the double
feature of *I Love a Soldier* and *A Night of Adventure*.
Maybe we were letting our eyeball-loads of Paulette God-
dard succumbing to Sonny Tufts settle a little, maybe we
were merely gawking at a Phoenix of streets tightpacked
with cars nose to tail like an endless elephant review
and of sidewalks aswim with soldiers and fliers fifteen
thousand strong from the twenty bases in the desert
around; we had not seen much of cities, let alone a city
in fever. Either case, here the three of us onlook, until
my mother happens to send her eyes higher into the
night. "Charlie, Ivan. Look how pretty, what they've
put up." She points to the top of the Westward Ho Hotel.
Dad and I are as dazzled as she at the sign on the peak
of the tall building, stupendous jewelry of a quarter-
moon with a bright star caught on its horn. We peer up
at the design, trying to fathom the perfectly achieved
silverghost illumination, until my father ventures, "Ye
know, I think those are real." We forge a few feet ahead
on the crammed sidewalk to test this and sure enough,
moon and star go trapezing upward from the hotel roof

to hang on sky—not an advertising inspiration after all, but the planet Venus and the ripening moon in rare conjunction.

On such a night, the fresh zodiac of Arizona must have seemed just what my parents were looking for after their recent Montana struggles. We all recalled Christmas as a rough spot on the calendar, but now it was healful 1945, February in fact, next thing to high summer in this palmy climate. Lately at Alcoa the management had realized how rare were undraftable colorblind 43-year-olds who knew how to run a crew, and my father came zinging home from the plant newly made a foreman. Before my mother could assemble our promising news off to Wally on his Pacific vessel, though, the ink turned to this:

His stomach bothers him all the time. He is so thin. I'm worried to death about Charlie.

Always before, it took something the calibre of getting tromped beneath a bucking horse to lay Charlie Doig out. But this ulcer deal . . . how could a gastric squall put my whangleather father on the couch, sick as a poisoned pup?

My father being my father, he tensely urges my mother to relax, will she, about the situation: "Oh-hell-Berneta-I'll-be-okay-in-just-a-little-bit."

There that Sunday as my father tries to sleep away the volcano in his middle, my mother all of a sudden is alone. Anna and Joe are newly gone, called away by the death of Joe's father and obligations back in Montana. Busy in the rear yard and childhood, I am obliviously pushing my roads to the gates of Berlin and raining bombs onto Tokyo. Beyond 119B's windows, Alzona Park is entirely what it is built to be, war's warehouse of strangers. By instinct, not to say need, my mother goes to her companion the ink.

Dear Wally—

   . . . Somehow you seem to be a better pal than anyone else . . .

This first letter in the chain that Wally chose to save must have come aboard the *Ault* to him like her voice thrown around the world. Certainly that is what she is trying, quick as the pen will push through such afraid words as *worried to death*, such Alzona aloneness that *I have to spill over to someone*. Creed of all writers: *I have to*.

Noon wears past; a missed mealtime, unheard of in our family. Then the half hour and she still writes, does not awaken my father. Dares not. *If Charlie doesn't improve . . .*

Well, I better calm down, the lines to Wally work themselves wry. *If a censor reads this, he probably won't even let you get it.*

Taking to paper with that Sunday of worries about an abruptly ailing husband, my mother knowingly or not put her pen at the turning point in their marriage, their fates. The very reason we had catapulted ourselves to Arizona was because, always before, he was worried to death about her.

What I know of her is heard in the slow poetry of fact. The freight of name, Berneta Augusta Maggie Ringer, with its indicative family tension of starting off German and ending up Irish. Within the year after her birth in 1913 in Wisconsin, her parents made the one vaulting move they ever managed together and it was a whopper: in the earliest photo I have of my mother Berneta after the westward train deposited them in Montana, she is a toddler in a sunbonnet posed with a dead bear.

Ringer family life kept that hue, always someplace rough. Up in the Crazy Mountains, the bear lair, where Tom and Bessie Ringer and this infant daughter somehow survived a first Montana winter in a snow-banked tent while they skidded out lodgepole logs as paltry as their shelter. Then other jounces of job and shanty which finally landed them near the railroad village of Ringling. Off and on for the next thirty years, some shred of the family was in that vicinity to joke about being the Ringers of Ringling. It says loads in the story of my mother that a single syllable was utterly all those coincidental names had in common, for Ringling was derived from *the* Ringlings of circus baronage.

Was it some obscure Wisconsin connection—the Ringlings of Baraboo origins, the Ringers most lately from Wisconsin Rapids—or just more fate-sly coincidence, that brought about my grandparents' employment by the Ringlings? Maybe Dick Ringling, the circus brothers' nephew who ran the Montana side of things, was entertained by the notion that a millennium ago the families might have been cousins across a medieval peat bog. By whatever whim, hired they were, and the Ringers began their milky years at Moss Agate.

Not exactly a ranch, even less a farm, Moss Agate flapped on the map as a loose end of circusman John Ringling's landholdings in the Smith River Valley of south-central Montana. Sagebrushy, high, dry, windy; except for fingernail-sized shards of cloudy agate, the place's only natural resource was railroad tracks. When he bought heavily into the Smith River country John Ringling had built a branch line railroad to the town of White Sulphur Springs and about midway along that twenty-mile set of tracks happened to be Moss Agate, although you would have to guess hard at any of that now. Except for a barn which tipsily refuses to give in to gravity, Moss Agate's buildings are vanished, as is John Ringling's railroad, as is the Chicago, Milwaukee & St. Paul transcontinental railroad which Ringling's line branched onto. At the time, though, around the start of the nineteen-twenties, John Ringling and his nephew Dick saw no reason why all those vacant acres shouldn't set them up as dairy kings. They built a vast barn at White Sulphur Springs, loaded up with milk cows, and stuck the leftovers in satellite herds at places such as Moss Agate with hired milkers such as the Ringers.

There is one particularly bitter refrain of how my mother's family fared at Moss Agate: the cow stanza. From Wisconsin arrived a trainload of the dairy cattle, making a stop at the Moss Agate siding en route to the ballyhooed new biggest-barn-west-of-the-Mississippi-River at White Sulphur Springs. Grandly the Ringers were told to select the excess herd they would run for the Ringlings. The cows turned out to be culls, the old and halt and lame from the dairylots of canny Wisconsin. My grandfather and grandmother tried to choose a boxcarload that looked like the least wretched, and the Ringling honchos began unloading the new Moss Agate herd for them. Not clear is whether the cows were simply turned loose by the Ringling men or broke away, but in either case cows erupted everywhere, enormous bags and teats swinging from days of not having been milked, moo-moaning the pain of those overfull udders, misery on the hoof stampeding across the sage prairie while away chugged the train to White Sulphur to begin Dick Ringling's fame as a dairy entrepreneur. Even the frantic roundup that Tom and Bessie Ringer were left to perform was not the final indignity; Moss Agate at the time did not yet provide that woozy barn or even any stanchions, so the herd had to be snubbed down by lariats, cow after ornery kicky cow, for milking.

The Ringlings could afford Montana as a hobby; the Ringers were barely clinging to the planet. My grandfather Tom seems to have been one of those natural bachelors who waver into marriage at middle age and never quite catch up with their new condition. My grandmother Bessie, I know for sure, was a born endurer who would drop silently furious at having to take on responsibility beyond her own, then go ahead and shoulder every last least bit of it. Certainly over time their marriage became a bone-and-gristle affair that matched the Moss Agate country they were caught in. Nonetheless, child after child after child: Paul, then Bud, then Wally. My mother had reached five years old when the first of this brother pack came along, so she was steadily separate by a span or two of growing-up; veteran scholar at the one-room schoolhouse by the time the boys had to trudge into the first grade, willowing toward womanhood while they still mawked around flinging rocks at magpies. The shaping separateness of Berneta within the Ringer family, however, did not spring simply from being the eldest child and the only daughter. No, nothing that mere. Another knotting rhythm of fact: she slept always with three pillows propping her up, angle akin to a hospital bed, so that she could breathe past the asthma.

To this day, people will wince when they try to tell me of asthma's torture of my mother. Most often a midnight disorder, sabotage of sleep and dream that had just decently begun, the attack would choke her awake, simultaneously the blue narcotic of carbon dioxide buildup bringing on faintness, a suffocating fatigue. At once she had to fight to sit up and wheeze, her eyes large with concentration on the cost of air, hunching into herself to ride out the faltering lungwork. In and out, the raw battlesound of debilitation and effort sawed away at her. Then worse: a marathon of coughing so hard it bruised you to hear. The insidious breath shortage could go on for hours. Medication, inhalers, alleviation of any true sort waited a generation or so into the future. When my grandparents stared down into a Wisconsin cradle and for once agreed with each other that they had to take this smothering child to the drier air of the West, they gave her survival but not ease.

She first comes to me, naturally, by pen. *There are many disadvantages to farming in some parts of Montana . . .* The earliest item from her own hand is a grade school booklet she made about Montana, report of a forthright rural child. *Some times there is alkali ground and in other places gumbo soil and then the chinook winds and grasshoppers and all different kinds of insects and some times not enough rainfall.* Language is the treasury of the

poor, and Berneta minted more than her share even in
the busy-tongued Ringer family—*fee-fee* was her saying
of barefoot, anything spooky brought on not the willies
but *the jimjams*, and she it was who coined for the family
the marvelous eartrick *merseys* for Moss Agate's Jersey-
cows-in-need-of-mercy. Phrases were dressed up for fun,
any dark cloud *commencing to look like rain*, any fancy
angler categorized as having *his face hung out as a fisher-
man*. Emphasis had a vocabulary all its own in this youngster. Riding her horse as fast as it could be made to go
was *full slam*. Her father patching the Moss Agate roof,
which always needed it to the utmost, was Papa tarring
the life out of it. When a chance at something, such as a
trip to town, was seized upon, it was *glommed on to*. Hard
luck, though, was *a bum go*.

And so I wonder. Do I meet my own mother, young,
in the experiences of Western women who endured a
land short of everything but their own capacities? Is her
favorite school subject of Latin—the *gravitas* of declen-
sions as a refuge, as it was for me—prefigured in well-
spoken Kathryn Donovan, teacher of all eight grades at
the sagebrush-surrounded Moss Agate school? Did she
take to heart, sometime when she visited the Norwegian
family tucked over the hill from Moss Agate, gaunt
Mary Brekke's immigrant anthem of "You better learn!"
that marched Brekke child after child into educated good
citizenship? Such civic women are caryatids of so much
of that hard Montana past, they carry the sky. Yet I find
it not enough to simply count her into their company.
Too many pictures of this familiar-faced stranger say she
was dangerously more complicated than that, she cannot
be sculpted from sugar.

Instead: from photo after photo with shacky Moss Agate or marginal Ringling in the background, Berneta Ringer assembles herself as someone not growing out of childhood but simply flinging it off, refusing to lose time to the illness in herself. *Sick of being sick*, she'd surely have said it, time and again she pals with a crowd of cowboy hats and Sunday frocks in the pose of a person out and launched in life—but when I interrogate time and place, I realize I am looking at five feet of uncorked teenager. Some dreams, mostly of the daylight sort, we are able to aim; the motion of Berneta's mind often was horseback, her saddle-straddling generation finding its freedom in the ride to Saturday night dances and two- or three-day Fourth of July rodeos. Right there, perhaps, is where the female rural youngsters of the twenties parted from the generation of their mothers, in riding astride to those dances with a party dress tied behind the saddle; or as in Berneta's case in the photo taken when she can have been barely fifteen, mounting a rodeo cowboy's horse in her flapper dress and cloche hat, her high heels flagrantly snug in the stirrups.

This teenage Berneta, then, has the strange independence of a comet, a pushed pitch of existence that makes her seem always beyond her numerical age. In every camera-caught mood, wide-set eyes soft but with a minimum of illusions: on the verge of pretty but perfectly well aware she's never going to get there past the inherited broad nose. Wally's face was a borrowed coin of hers, with that enlivened best-friend quality from the central slight overbite which parted the lips as if perpetually interested and about to ask. But her query breathes up from the album page not as Wally's romping *ready to go?* but the more urgent *how do I keep life from being a bum go?* What comes out most of all, whether the camera catches her as an inexplicable pixie in a peaked cap or gussied up as a very passable flapper, is that whenever she had enough oxygen, Berneta burned bright.

The most haunting photograph I possess of my mother is a tableau of her on horseback, beneath a wall of rock across the entire sky behind her. This is not Moss Agate but higher bolder country, and she has costumed herself up to it to the best of her capacity. She wears bib overalls, a high-crowned cowgirl hat, and leather chaps with MON-TANA spelled out in fancy rivets down the leg-length and a riveted heart with initials in it putting period to the tidings. The mountain West as a stone rainbow, a girl-turning-woman poised beneath it.

Enter the Doigs, at a gallop.

Once, on a government questionnaire which asked a listing of "racial groups within community," back from the Doigs' end of the county sailed the laconic enumeration, "Mostly Scotch." The country out there toward Sixteenmile Creek even looked that way, Highlandish, intemperate. Certainly the Doigs inhabited it in clan quantity: six brothers and a sister, with aunts and uncles and cousins and double cousins up every coulee. Above the basin in the Big Belt Mountains where the family homestead-stretched-into-a-ranch was located sat a tilted crown of rimrock called Wall Mountain, and my father and the other five Doig boys honed themselves slick

against that hard horizon. A generation after the steam-
ship crossed the Atlantic, they spoke with a Dundee burr
and behaved like test pilots.

A dance, of course, did the trick; began the blinding
need of my mother and my father for each other. When
the Saturday night corps of Claude and Jim and Angus
and Red and Ed and Charlie Doig hit a dance at the
rail villages of Ringling or Sixteen or any of the rural
schoolhouses between, the hall at once colored up into
a plaid of bandannaed gallantry and hooty mischief—
wherever you glanced, the Doig boys would be taking
turns doing the schottische with their widowed mother
and jigging up a storm with their girlfriends, not to
mention wickedly auditing their sister Anna's potential
beaus whether or not she wanted them audited. Amid
this whirl of tartan cowboys, the one to watch is the
shortest and dancingest, a goodlooking jigger of a man
built on a taper down from a wide wedge of shoulders to
wiry tireless legs. There at the bottom, newbought Levi's
are always a mile too long for Charlie Doig but he rolls
them up into stovepipe cuffs, as if defiantly declaring he
fills out a pair of pants in every way that really counts.
The rhythm of his life is the chancy work of ranches,
which began in bronc riding that left him half dead a
couple of times and which he has persevered past to
shoulder into respect as a foreman of crews, and Saturday
night entitles him to cut loose on a hall floor with slickum
on it. Charlie in his habits is the fundamental denomina-
tor of the Doig boys, saddle scamps who also have a
reputation for working like blazes. Customarily after
these rural nightfuls of music and other intoxicants, people wobble home for too few hours' sleep before groaning

up to milk the cow or feed the sheep or other dismally looming chores. But the Doig boys, whatever their state, fly at the chores the minute they reach home and sleep uninterrupted after. The double energy it takes to be a practical thrower of flings is concentrated here in Charlie, built like a brimming shotglass. This time, this Saturday night of fling, when the square-dance caller chants out to the gents *dosiedoe, and a little more doe*—well, there stands Berneta.

Promisingly full of bad intentions, my tuned-up father must have been just what my mother was trying to figure out how to order. Boundaries of dream take human shape, there when our bodies begin their warm imagining. But beyond the welcoming geography of the first touch of each other in the small of the back as the two of them danced together stood twenty horseback miles between the Doig place and Moss Agate. My father being my father, he simply made up his mind to treat that as virtually next door. Berneta Ringer and her newly given fountain pen reciprocated. My grandmother would tell me decades later, still more than a little exasperated at the fact, that she could never set foot off Moss Agate without having to mail another batch of Berneta's letters to Charlie Doig. "If that's who she wanted, I couldn't do any other."

So. There was ink, ink, ink then too, trying to speak the moments of my parents' earlier wartime, the battle toward marriage. (My mother's youngness and tricky health were in the way, my father's sense of obligation at the struggling Doig property was in the way, everybody's finances, or dearth of, were in the way.) The box curtains of the mind: we never fully imagine, let alone believe in, what was said to one another by those impossible beings, our parents before they were our parents. Yet I overhear enough in her later letters, Wally's packet, for an educated guess that those Moss Agate pages crackled with diagnosis of her and my father and those they knew. How soft-voiced she was, I am always told; so the snow angel outline everyone has given me of my mother luckily takes a devilish edge when she puts on paper for Wally such gossip as *the jam Little Miss Buckshot got herself in. Married to 3 soldiers and no divorces, & getting allotments from all three. She was doing alright until the F.B.I. caught up with her.* Entire plot of a novel tattled there, I note with professional admiration. What Berneta found to say by mail to her cowboy suitor, my father, surely had similar salt in the tenderness.

He gave back the tense hum of a wire in the wind. Charlie Doig coming courting sang several lives at once, a number of them contradictions. In that dependable square-lined face it could be read that there was much inward about him, a tendency to muse, dwell on things; and yet as the saying was, you could tell a lot about a guy by the way he wore his hat and Charlie always wore his cocked. A delicious talker when he wasn't busy, but he was busy all the time too. Temper like a hot spur, yet with plenty of knack to laugh at himself. Bantam-legged as he was, he practically ran in search of work, forever whanging away at more than one job at a time, in lambing or calving or haying on the valley's big ranches and meanwhile pitching in with the other Doig brothers to try to make a go of the family livestock holdings at Wall Mountain, during Montana's preview of the Depression. Such exertions sometimes tripped across each other, as when Berneta threw a birthday party for him and he was detoured by a bronc that broke his collarbone. "I could've sent the horse," she was notified by him from the hospital, "he was healthy enough." It didn't matter then to my adoring mother-to-be, but how could a man that whimsical be so high-strung, how could a man so high-strung be so full of laughing? In and out of his share of Saturday night flirtations, this lively veteran singleton might have been counted on to kiss and move on. But he contradicted contradictions. From that first night of dancing in Ringling, my father's attachment to the half-frail half-vital young woman at Moss Agate flamed so long and strong that in the end it must be asked if his, too, didn't constitute an incurable condition.

The brusque sagebrush would slap at your stirrups, polishing the leather at the bottoms of your chaps, if you rode their country yet today.

Sage like a dwarf orchard, climbing with the land as the valley around Moss Agate swells west into ridges, then cascades toward Sixteenmile Creek in more and more hills, a siege of hills.

Except where dominated by Wall Mountain and Grass Mountain, the higher horizon now begins to repeat those tough anonymous foothills in summits that bulge up one after another in timbered sameness.

This Sixteen country is a cluttered back corner of the West where the quirky Big Belt Mountains are overshadowed by the grander Bridger range immediately to the south. From the air over the Big Belts, the nature of their oddly isolated sprawl becomes evident. Not particularly lofty, not especially treacherous in skyline, not much noticed in history except for the long-ago goldstrike at Confederate Gulch, this wad of unfamous mountains nonetheless stands in the way of everything major around them. They haze the Missouri River unexpectedly north-west from its headwaters for about ninety miles before the flow can find a passage around their stubborn barrier and down the eastern slope of the continent. By one manner of geologic reckoning, the main range of the Rocky Mountains ends, a little ignominiously, east of Townsend where the mudstone and limestone perimeters of the Big Belts begin. Across on the Smith River Valley side of the Big Belt range, the steady plains of mid-Montana receive a rude bump upward to a valley-*floor* elevation of 5,280 feet. Goblin canyons chop in and out of the sixty-five-mile frontage of the Big Belts, but a scant two give any route through: Deep Creek Canyon where the highway has been threaded between snowcatch-ing cliffs, and the Sixteen Canyon, graveyard of railroad ventures.

Not immediately obvious territory to find delight in. Yet my parents' honeymoon summer on Grass Mountain wed them to this particular body of earth.

The two of them had decided to defy the Depression's laws of gravity, and in 1934, when she was twenty and he thirty-three, they married and went herding sheep on Grassy.

Again according to our family diarist, the Brownie box camera, that set of months agreed with Charlie and Berneta Doig, an uncomplicated shirtsleeves-rolled-up summertime of following the sheep—my mother slender as filament, my father jauntily at home at timberline.

Grass Mountain itself, a pleasant upsidedownland with timber at its base and meadows across its summit, gave my parents elevation of more than one kind. Their summer on Grassy was a crest of the rising and falling seasonal rhythm that they were now to follow through life together in Montana.

By then my father had tugged himself up by the ropes of his muscles and the pulleys of his mind to where he could take charge of a season, generally summer. This took some doing, too, given where he had to start from. Pieces of the past stay on as pieces of us, do they? My father came out of the candlelight of this century, born in the spring of 1901 back there on the homestead beneath Wall Mountain. More than that, born on the losing side of America's second civil war, the one out west where dollars were the big battalions. That Western Civil War of Incorporation, the businesslike name given it by its leading historian, powerfully pitted financial capital and government against those who occupied land or jobs in inconvenient unconsolidated fashion. Indian tribes and Hispanos: defeated onto reservations and into poverty's enclaves. Miners, loggers and other industrial working stiffs: defeated in strikes and resistance to technological dangers. Homesteaders, small farmers, backpocket ranchers: defeated from insufficient acres. The lariat proletariat, where my grandparents and parents started out, was done in by mechanization, ending up in town jobs or none. As the Doig place and all other smallholdings in the Sixteen country gradually folded their colors, my father by necessity worked his way out and while he was at it, up. In the June to September season that was the heart of Montana ranching, he could take a herd of cattle

or a band of sheep into the mountains for their owner
and bring them into the shipping pen fat and profitable,
or he could just as deftly oversee other ranch hands as a
camptender or foreman, or he could even hire a crew of
his own on a haying contract from a rancher glad enough
to pay him by the ton to take care of the whole long
aggravating job of putting up hay. There were summers
when he did two out of the three, always on the go under
his work-stained Stetson and behind the jaw he jutted at
the horizon.

Up only went so far, though. Montana's vast wheel
of seasons always had a flat, skewed side—the biggest
side—and that was winter. You could thud pretty hard
in autumn, too, and before spring managed to definitely
get on track. For year-round ranching, even a go-getter
needed an extensive piece of inherited land or a hefty
family wallet or a father-in-law with deep pockets. None
of which Charlie Doig had been put on this earth with,
and he well knew it. "As the fellow says," I hear his burr
coming, "where's all the wherewithal?"

So, a summer on a mountain that shouted its name in
grass, with a bride both new and long-awaited at his side,
must have made a high season indeed for my father. No
question about it for my mother, either. I know—have
seen for myself in the years beyond hers—how the elevation there on Grassy opens up the view of the closed-away
Sixteen country, diminishes the relentless sage and the
raw shale cutbanks and the pinched gulches where failed
homesteads are pocketed away, and takes the eye instead
toward the neighboring and more generous Bridger
Mountains; and just before the Bridgers, the one cocky
tilt in the nondescript Big Belts, Wall Mountain. The

imagination is easily led down past Wall Mountain's inclined rimrock to the canyon of Sixteenmile Creek, as ornery for its size as any chasm anywhere. The first railroad that was squeezed through there required fifty-eight bridges in eighteen miles. Enough floods and avalanches, plus an earthquake or two, and the Sixteen Canyon spat out both that first railroad and the subsequent Chicago, Milwaukee & St. Paul transcontinental line. Not a rail, not a tie, is left on the scar of roadbed, but the rattlesnakes that the railroad maintenance men hung on the right-of-way fence as sarcastic trophies are back in force. I always have a feeling, along those lines, about this original America of the Doigs, this Sixteen country and these Big Belt Mountains: one moment, the look of the land strongly stops you in your tracks, and the next, there is something ominous around your ankles. We were expected to grow used to it, I suppose, as Scotch endurers, as cockleburr American highlanders. But what am I to make of my mother's embrace of all this? Unlike me, unlike my father, she was not born into this chancy Sixteen country. She came as a convert. For, of course, that proudest photo of her, rhinestone cowgirl beneath the stone rainbow, that photo was taken at Wall Mountain, summit of the Sixteen country.

After their 1934 summer of herding, my parents went on into a skein of ranch jobs together, my mother cooking for whatever crew my father was running. But ranch wages were always thin coin. Settled down now, comparatively, into marriage, my father felt he had to turn his hand to operating a place "on shares," which was to say running somebody's ranch for them for a cut of each year's profit. The center years of my parents' story together come now at the hem of Grass Mountain, the first years of World War Two when the pair of them took the Faulkner Creek ranch on shares.

A scrape of road pierced through that sagebrush of the Sixteen country toward Wall Mountain until suddenly making a veer toward Grassy, and the Faulkner Creek drainage.

Not paying much attention to the rest of the world or each other, the ornery mountains of the Big Belts did hold pockets of ranchcraft for people as acquainted with work as my parents were. For better or worse, a place such as Faulkner Creek met them on its own clear terms. A tidy sum of rangeland without being elbowy about it, with plump hayfields and the creek almost at the front door, that ranch in a majority of ways represented what the Doig homestead could only ever be the kernel of or the Moss Agate tenancy a gaunt ghost of. A do-it-yourself expanse, the West was supposed to be and rarely is. The makings were there at Faulkner Creek, if you were nimble enough and canny enough and stubborn enough and enough other enoughs, to profitably handle a thousand sheep or a couple hundred cattle year in and year out. My parents filled the bill. The Sixteen country was their business address, they knew it like Baruch did Wall Street.

So they also knew about the isolation, more than twenty miles to town and most of that simply to reach a paved road, which they were going to have to put up with at Faulkner Creek. Polarly remote a couple of seasons of the year, it was the kind of ranch, in my mother and father's saying for it, where you had to be married to the place. Two other ranches lay hidden even farther down the gulches of Sixteen Creek and Battle Creek, but otherwise weather was the only neighbor. Clouds walking the ridgelines, hurried by chilly wind. Rain, rare as it was, slickening the road as quick as it lit. And if the winter was a tough one—they always were—my father fed hay on the road so that as the sheep ate, they packed down the snow and improved the chance of getting out to the hospital at Townsend when one of my mother's hardest asthma attacks hit.

I will always have to wonder whether some of the distances in myself come from starting life there beside Faulkner Creek. My parents had greatly hoped for twins, but instead got the mixture that was me. Maybe the medical stricture that one pregnancy was plenty for my mother to risk, that after I eventuated into the picture in the summer of 1939 there were going to be no sisters or brothers for me, made my parents allow me into the adult doings of the ranch. As far back as memory will take me, I liked that; honorary membership with the grownups, admittance to their talk. It does give you the habit from early on, though, of standing back and prowling with your ears.

Definitely I was doted on. My mother's photo album contains a flurry of my uncles holding me atop horses until, probably when I was between three and four years old, there I sit in the worldly saddle by myself and handle the reins as if I know what I'm doing. By then, too, World War Two and its songs on the radio had come, and I was the combination of kid who could listen to *mairzy doats and dozy doats, and little lambsie divy*, and staidly tell you, sure, everybody knows mares eat oats and a doe could too, and lambs would take to ivy; then go outside and disappear into fathoms of imagination the rest of the day. Touchy and thorough, doctrinaire and dreamy, healthy as a moose calf, I seem to have sailed through the Faulkner Creek years with my adults giving to me generously from their days. Words on a page became clear to me there, long before school; somebody in the revolving cast of busy parents and young Ringer uncles hired to do the ranch chores and a visiting grandmother checking up on us from Moss Agate, one or another of those had to have been steadily reading to me. My immersion into print, the time indoors with books and a voice willing to teach me all the words, surely I owe to that ranch's long winters.

Winter also brought out the trapper, to be watched from our kitchen window in the snow-roofed ranch house, tending the trapline on Faulkner Creek.

The bundled figure sieves in and out of the creekside willows, a dead jackrabbit in hand for bait. Gray to catch white, for weasels in their snowy winter coats are the quarry, their pelts fetching a prime price from the fur buyer in Helena.

The weasels hunt along the creek in invisibility against the snow, terror to grouse and mice, or dart up to the ranch buildings, murder in the chickenhouse; their sylph bodies are such ferocious little combustion tubes that they have to eat with feverish frequency to live. Wherever the double dots of weasel tracks indicate, the trapper sets a small contraption of jaws and trigger and neatly baits it with a bloody morsel of rabbit. Ritual as old as any tribe—though these traps are springsteel, bought from a catalogue—but every trapper possesses a trademark and this one distinctively takes the trouble to bend a bow of branch in attachment to each trap. When the animal sets off the trap, the branch will yank the entire apparatus up into the cold air and the weasel will die a quicker, less contorted death.

One after another the traps are attended to this way, an even dozen in all. The trapsetting impulse evidently is the same as in catching fish, the snarer hates to quit on an odd number.

Not nearly all the visited traps hold weasels this day but enough do, each frozen ermine form dropped in careful triumph into the gunnysack at the trapper's waist. At last, from the end of the trapline the figure turns back up the creek, again toward the ranch house with the meringue of snow on its roof. The trapper is my mother.

Her sharp-aired victories over asthma, an hour at a time there on her trapline while my father sat sentinel with me at the kitchen window, were one calendar of the Faulkner Creek years. Another was my father's rhythm of mastering the ranch. The livestock in his canny rotation of pastures, the hayfields encouraged by his irrigating shovel, a ranch hand or two deployed at fence-fixing or other upkeep, all responded to the zip he brought to the place. Faulkner Creek's wicked road showed a bright side here; the ranch owner from Helena didn't chance out to the place very often, and good thing that he didn't. My father could run something as everyday as a ranch fine and dandy. What he refused to regulate was his lifelong opinion of bosses. "Can ye imagine that Helena scissorbill wanting me to put the upper field into alfalfa? The sheep'd get into that and bloat to death until Hell couldn't hold them. A five-year-old kid—Ivan here—knows better than that."

One more mark of my parents' aiming-upward-but-allegiant-in-other-directions was the Ford. Our snappy sky blue 1940 coupe, fat-fendered and long-hooded, a good two-thirds of the car prowing ahead of us as we fought the Faulkner Creek road. What the four of us, my mother and father and I and the Ford, are most remembered for is the ritual of washing before a funeral. Parked in the middle of a creek crossing, we would peel off our shoes and socks, my father and I would roll up our pants legs and my mother would safety-pin her dress into a culotte and out we would step into the pebbled water. I was given a rag and granted the hubcaps to wash, the steel circles like four cleansed moons rising from the creekwater. My father and mother went to work on the greater grit, mud caked on the fenders, bug splatters on the hood, the Ford gradually but dependably coming clean under tossed bucketsful of rinse. Ready now for the drive behind the hearse, we headed on into White Sulphur Springs, where the deceased actually do go a last mile from town out to the cemetery. The men who were to be buried, for they almost always were men, were the hired hands of the Big Belt country who had worked with my parents at haying, lambing, calving—people who drew no cortege while they were alive. People with a wire down somewhere in their lives, a lack of capacity to work for themselves, an emigration into an America they never managed to savvy nor to let go of, many with a puppy-helplessness when it came to alcohol, some with sour tempers and bent minds; mateless. At any of these funerals, my mother most likely would be the only woman there. Neither my mother nor my father could have said so in words, but in that wiping away of the mud and dust from the Ford coupe's fenders and flanks—that handling of the country—was a last chore to mark those other chore-filled lives.

Faulkner Creek was no closer to Eden than it was anywhere else, but by every family fragment of that time and place my parents seemed to be in their element. Camera shots again say so, most of all in the trophy pictures from the war with the coyotes.

Sunny day, icicles starting to shrink upward to the log eaves of the ranch house. Everybody has paraded around the corner of the house to take a pose with the vanquished coyotes.

My mother, especially pert in one of her striped house-dresses and only a short jacket.

My visiting grandmother even hardier, out there in apron and bare arms.

My mother's second youngest brother Bud on hand as our hired man, in dutiful earflap cap.

Then my father and his rifle and me.

Since I, little Mr. Personality in a brass-button snow-suit, appear to be not quite a three-year-old, the photo likely dates from near the end of the winter of 1941–42. This scene speaks in several ways. First of all, the extraordinary statement of the coyotes around and above my father and me as we pose, twenty-eight of them in simultaneous leap of death up the log wall where their pelts are strung. Winterlong they had been picked off, for the safety of the sheep and the sake of bounty, as they loped

the open ridges above Faulkner Creek; ideal coyote country, but unluckily for them, also ideal coyote-hunting
country for somebody who could shoot like my father.
Next, it always comes as a pleasant shock, how on top of
life my father looks in this picture. Forty years and jobs
after his start on the doomed Wall Mountain homestead,
bounty of all kinds seems to be finding him at last. Posed
there, he is in command not just of one season a year but
a prospering ranch, he knows of at least twenty-eight
coyotes who will give his sheep no further trouble, he
has a son and heir, his coveted wife is taking the photo
of this moment, a winter-ending chinook has arrived
with this sun—a day of thaw, truly.

My own farthest pattern of memory is the Faulkner
Creek ranch's generator—the light plant, we called the
after-dark engine, throbbing diesel factory of watts—as
it hammered combustion into the glow of kitchen and
living room bulbs. The light plant was used sparingly,
like sparks put to tinder when the cave most needed
dazzle; when company dropped in, say. And so the yam-
mer of it in the night-edge of my mind must be from a
few of my recalcitrant bedtimes, boy determined not to
waste awakeness while luscious light was being made.

But why that diesel monotony of echo?

Why not the toss of wind in the restless pine that
overleaned the ranch house, or a coyote's night-owning
anthem?

Why persistently hear, even now in the rhythms of
my writing keys working, the *puh puh puh* labor of that
light plant?

Because in every way, this was the pulse of power coming into our rural existence. Not simply the tireless stutter of electrical generation but the sound of history turning. We had only a diesel tidbit of it there at Faulkner Creek and my parents were of the relic world of muscle-driven tasks, yet, like passersby magnetized out of our customary path, power now made its pull on us. One of the great givens of World War Two manufacture was that power could kettle an ore called bauxite into bomberskin called aluminum.

Out of those particles, those waves, this first deliberate dream.

The heavy rain on Christmas Eve of 1944 is contradicting my mother's notion of what both Christmas and Phoenix ought to be. She is trying to work the mood to death, baking an army of cookies and rapidly wrapping Anna and Joe's presents (filmy kerchief for her, carton of cigarettes for him) while they're out visiting friends they know from Montana, and naturally the weather is keeping me inside, which is to say in her hair, until she puts me to crayoning a festive message to my grandmother. I come up with MERRY CHRISTMAS GRANDMA in the countless fonts of my printed handwriting and devote the rest of the page to dive-bombers blowing up everything in sight.

The outside door rattles open, solving the whereabouts of my father, late from the aluminum plant this night of all nights. But his inevitable approximate whistling of "The Squaws Along the Yukon" doesn't follow on in to the front room. All of a sudden he is in the kitchen with my mother and me, checking us over with his sheepcounting look even though we can only tally up to two. Puts his lunchbox down. Goes to the silverware drawer, takes out a tableknife, heads back to the front room where he jams the blade into the crack under the doorway casing so that the knife snugs the door unopenable. (Whatever this is about, Anna and Joe are in for a surprise when they come home and try to get in.) He zips back into the kitchen, pours himself a cup from the constant coffeepot and begins his news ever so casually, as he likes to do.

"Did ye happen to hear?"

I have only one fact in me—that it's about to be Christmas—and my mother but two—that it's about to be Christmas and we are an interplanetary distance from anybody and anywhere we know—and so my father's bulletin arrives spectacularly fresh. Leave it to him, he has pried it out of one of the aluminum plant gate guards who were giving everybody a going-over at tonight's change of shifts, making the entire workgang shuffle through in single-file so their security badges could be hawkishly inspected.

"A whole hell of a bunch of German prisoners got away," is the report my father brings. The great breakout at the Papago Park prisoner of war camp had been engineered by U-boat men, tunnel-visioned in the most effective sense: somehow they dug through a couple of feet of hardpan a day for the past three months, and tonight twenty-five of them have moled out to freedom, under the cover of ruckus set up by their comrades. "They're watching for the buggers everywhere."

Including, now, 119B.

"What's next in the stampede," murmurs my mother, simply in commentary of German POWs added to the rest of the deluge out there. Tonight she wouldn't be surprised if the moon itself came squashing down on Phoenix.

Meanwhile I am scared, flabbergasted, and inspired. *A tunnel!* A foxhole is nothing compared to that; tomorrow will not be too soon for me to start my sandhog future beneath Alzona Park.

Huns at the door of Phoenix don't faze my father, at least with a caseknife jamming that door. He kids my mother about the Gluns and Zettels on her side of the family, "Just remember, Berneta, if the MPs come around here you're not related to those sauerkraut cousins of yours back in Wisconsin."

What? *What?* I'd done my teething on the war, could never remember when the grown-ups were not inveighing against Japs and Krauts. And now—

"Mama? Are we *Germans?*"

My mother shoots my father a now-look-what-you've-started look. "We're pedigreed Scotch," he assures me, but can't resist adding: "Even you and Mama—ye both caught it from me."

I am determined to get this matter of breed straight. "How did we catch it?"

My father gives the handsome jaunty grin off the Grass Mountain photographs. "It got pretty contagious there for a while."

Naturally I want to follow up on that, but my mother, business to do with cookies and wrapping paper, pokes another look at my father. "Do you figure you're about done stirring him up?"

"I guess maybe so," he acknowledges as he studies her. "Now what can I do about you?" All at once he says, so soberly it breaks on the air as a kind of plea:

"Merry damn Christmas, Berneta."

Realization lifts her upper lip in the middle, her index of surprise. She honestly hasn't known how much her mood has been showing. She is at a loss. "Charlie, I only—"

She hunches her shoulders a little, smallest shrug, but on it ride all the distances of this Christmas. Not only is my mother ten hundred miles separate from her own mother and father, they have separated from each other—my grandmother is cooking on a ranch in another part of Montana from Moss Agate and my grandfather is in parts unknown. Bounced like dice against the war's longitudes and latitudes, Wally is somewhere in the Pacific, my army uncle Paul is in Australia, here we are in aluminized Arizonan Alzona. This sunward leap of ours has been my father's doing, for my mother's sake. More and more spooked by her asthma battles in the isolation of the Faulkner Creek ranch, he flung the place away, piloted us out of Montana on war-bald tires and waning ration books, recast himself from ranchman into aluminum worker, he has desperately done what he thought there was to do, made the move to Arizona for the sake of health. For her sake. But he can see the immense journey unraveling here on the snag of Christmas, homesickness, out-of-placeness, and now he is looking the plea to her, everything gathered in his eyes pulling the square lines of his face tight.

Fuss about her health has always put a crowbar in my

mother's spine and it does again now. She straightens up as if shedding this hard year. She tells my father all the truth she has at the moment.

"I'll try to get over this, Charlie."

She takes a breath as big as she is, not an asthma gasp but just fuel for what she needs to put across to him about her isolation amid a cityful of strangers, how she misses everything about Montana there is to miss.

"It's going to take some trying," she lets him know.

Invisible in plain sight at the kitchen table, crayoned combat forgotten on the tablet paper in front of me, I watch back and forth at these gods of my world in their confusion.

At last my father nods to my mother and says as though something has been settled: "That's all we can any of us do, Berneta, is try."

The escaped Germans do not devour us in our Christmas Eve beds—hightailing it to nonbelligerent Mexico seems more what they had in mind—and so we climb out to the day itself and its presents. Up out of the fiber of that boy who became me, can't my Christmas gift prospects be readily dreamed? Tricycle? Toy truck? Wicked new shovel? No, beyond any of those. Threadbare Alzona Park presented an actual item more magical than imagined ones can ever be. From out beyond the world's possibilities, I have been given—

The *Ault*.

Blessed conspiracy of Wally and my mother, this; he by mailing it in time and she by sneaking the gift wrapping onto this toy replica of his ship. Replica does not say it, really, because my *Ault* was tubby, basic—a flat-iron-sized vessel with a block of superstructure and a single droll dowel of cannon poking out, more like a Civil War ironclad than anything actually asteam in the United States Navy in 1944; but painted a perfect navy gravy gray, and there on the bow in thrilling authentication, the black lettering USS *Ault*. Wally would have had to go to the dictionary for *avuncular*, but he managed to give me a most benevolently unclelike warship.

Naturally the grown-ups have wasted Christmas on each other by giving dry old functional things back and forth, so while Anna and Joe and Dad and even my mother try to have what they think is a good time, my *Ault* and I voyage 119B all that day, past Gibraltars of chair legs, through the straits of doorways to the bays of beds. (All December the logbook of the actual *Ault* has been repeating an endless intonation—0440 COMMENCED ZIGZAGGING. 0635 CEASED ZIGZAGGING. 0645 RESUMED ZIGZAGGING—as the newly commissioned destroyer practiced the crazystitch that would advance day by day from Pearl Harbor to Tokyo Bay.) We make frequent weather reconnaissances to a window, for my mother has promised that if the rain ever stops we can breast the moistures of Arizona outside.

All the while, all this holiday, although I am not to know so until the letters return forty-two years later, my parents and I and Arizona are on Wally's mind. Along with my gift ship arrived his inquiry to my mother whether she thinks he would have any prospects where we are, after the war; are there flour mills and feed stores where he might land a trucking job?

Through us, like a signal tremor along a web strand, Phoenix is making itself felt even into the most distant Pacific. You can feel the growth thrust gathering (it undoubtedly is what my mother has been feeling), the postwar land rush coming when you can throw a doorknob on this desert and a dozen houses will sprout.

Yet my mother, glad as she would have been to have him on hand in our future, does not sing back what her favorite brother wants to hear.

As she was with my father, she will be doggedly honest with Wally, sending back to him that she really can't be sure how his chances would be here where I am dreamily *Ault*ing and where my father has brought our hopes.

There is plenty of Phoenix I haven't seen, she will write with pointblank neutrality.

Our story, my mother's, my father's, mine, would seem to need no help from imagination to predict us onward from that 1944 Christmas. Americans of our time lived some version of it by the hundreds of thousands, ultimate millions, as Phoenix's population greatened beyond those of Boston, Baltimore, Pittsburgh, Cleveland, Milwaukee, beyond that of entire states such as Montana, as America's center of gravity avalanched south to the Sunbelt. The picture of us-to-be is virtually automatic. My father doctors his way out of the ulcer siege, my mother's asthma stays subdued and her homesickness begins to ebb, we continue on as self-draftees in the sunward march of America. Sheepkeepers no more, now we be bombermakers. Naturalized Alzonans, no more or less ill-fitted for project living and eventual suburbs than any other defense work importees. As this last war winter drew down toward all that was going to burgeon beyond, we were right there at hand, ready-made, to install ourselves into the metropolis future that was Phoenix. Except we didn't.

WICKENBURG
MAR20
11-AM
1945
ARIZ.

Dear Wally—
I always thought a desert is just nothing,
but have changed my mind.

We two, my mother and I, navigate among the cacti. The road from the cabin threads in and out of any number of identical pale braids of wheel tracks, but we have memorized strategic saguaros, arms uplifted like green traffic policemen, at the turns we need to make. Behind the steering wheel of the Ford my mother keeps watch on the cloud-puffy March sky as much as she does our cactus landmarks. She hates bad roads (and has spent what seems like her whole life on them) but at least these of the desert are more sand than mud.

The odometer's little miles slowly go, three, seven, then ten and here is town, palm-sprigged Wickenburg. My mother believes she was not born to parallel-park, so she pulls around to a side street where the Ford can be nosed in and maybe escape notice.

On the round of town chores I tag along long-lipped at her side. First to the post office, with her letters ready to Wally (*We packed up and came to Wickenburg Mon. afternoon*), to my grandmother, to Anna and Joe and others in Montana. As ever, we don't receive quite as many as she sends.

No sooner are we onto the street again than I halt her with my news.

"Can you wait," she hypothesizes as parents always strangely do in public, "or do you have to go real bad?"

45

Crucially bad, I assure her.

My mother does not point out that I could have taken care of this when I had the entire Arizona desert to do it in, although she looks as if she might like to. We quickmarch to the street intersection, where she scans unfamiliar downtown Wickenburg. The sign she seeks does not display a bucking horse on a rampage the way it would in Montana, but at least it declares BUDWEISER. Into the saloon we troop. The bartender, sallow figure in sleeve garters, and my mother perched in the lastmost booth pretend each other aren't there as I trek to the M-E-N door.

The drugstore next. Among the sundries there, my mother's triumph is a scarce roll of film for her camera. After paying, she eyes me, gauging how far down in the dumps I am. "We better resort to ice cream cones," she determines.

Ice cream helps; when did it ever not? But my basic snit was rapidly back. I missed my father at every corner of each day, from his renegade pour of condensed milk into his breakfast coffee to turn it tan as his workshirt, until moonrise when he would burr his voice Scotcher than ever and tell me it was a braw bricht moonlicht nicht. My mother, all at once a single householder in a bareboard cabin ten miles out in the Sonoran desert, with everything there is on her mind, is doing her utmost to fill his absence, I know. But this situation of only one parent . . .

A carload of Phoenix people interrupts me in midmope by depositing themselves on the soda fountain stools with us. We learn from their jabbering to each other that they have driven sixty miles to see the snow on Yarnell Hill north of town, an excursion my blizzard-bred mother finds so comical that she sneaks a giggle to me between licks on her ice cream. Maybe we can go into the snowman business, my mother and I. If people jaunt from far Phoenix just to look upon snow, what might they pay for genuine mitten-made statuary of the stuff, snow fatsos mocking the saguaros.

Onward to groceries and the mumbo jumbo of ration stamps: Book Four reds, blue C2s, how many red points does butter take, good gosh, twenty-*four*?

Provisioned, more or less, we embark in the car again, my mother steering as if the traffic is a conspiracy concentrated against the Ford. Wickenburg is an intersection for everything—the Phoenix highway, the California highway, the highway north that we migrated down from Montana, that other earth. CABINSCafeCAFECabinsCAFE I watch the chant in neon as my mother conquers the hazards of Wickenburg's main street. The Hassayampa riverbed arrives beneath us, witchy leafless cottonwood trees along its banks. Our errand next is to retrieve some clean clothing from suitcases stashed at the edge-of-town boarding house where we stayed for a few nights before the desert cabin hove into our existence. How do we do it? In Wickenburg less than a week and already our belongings straddle two places.

Now we face our last destination in town, the one I hate so. My mother's expression is apprehensive, too, not to mention child-weary and chore-worn. (*A day is shot before I realize it*, she has confided to Wally of this go-it-alone treadmill.) As so often in the way she has had to live, this next chore of hers—ours—is medical.

Alongside her, up the savage steps I trudge, braw-bricht-moon-licht-nicht, the stairstep of chant does not work at all, I go from grumpy to downright cross. I was acquainted with hospitals, don't think I wasn't. In our Montana life my mother's worst asthma attacks meant pellmell dashes of the Ford into the night, my father rushing us through the black coil of Deep Creek Canyon to the hospital at Townsend, and then a day or two later, her breathing as regular as it ever became, my father and I would fetch her home from the hospital. Hospitals were where parents got substituted into altogether different beings: people who were sick.

Hallway, perpetually a hallway smelling hideously clean. Our footsteps make the hospital sound, doom doom. Now the room with the number on it, worse even than the smellhall . . .

My father is sitting in a chair as far as he can get from the hospital bed, fully dressed and with his stockman Stetson in his lap.

"The medical Jesus says I can go," he tells the two of us in the painted and polished way that only he can. "He claims it'll be the healthiest thing for me and him both if I clear out of here."

The cure for what had been ailing in my father turned out to be the roulette grace of fate. Here at Wickenburg pop up friends of ours, my parents' nearest neighbors from Montana, an older couple from the ranch next to the Faulkner Creek place. Like us, Allen and Winnie Prescott figured they'd had their fair share of blizzards in the Sixteen country, but very much unlike us, they possessed the family money and genteel level of life to have long since adopted the habit of wintering warm in Arizona. When we made the drive from Alzona Park one Sunday to call on these veteran snowbirds, the Prescotts cast one look at my skin-and-bones father and urged him to do some doctoring with a whiz of a physician they knew there in Wickenburg, they'd help us get settled, be on hand for whatever ensued. As soon as we packed up and removed to Wickenburg, the monthlong skewer of pain through the middle of my father proved to be not at all the chronic ulcer he'd been treated for in Phoenix, but an appendix seething toward rupture. The Wickenburg doctor hospitalized him on a Tuesday night, extracted the appendix the next morning, and now on Saturday was already turning the impatient patient loose to my mother and me. *That's what I call fast work*, her pen commends in relief.

This farfetched crossing of paths with the Prescotts probably saved my father's life and definitely it rescued my mother's mood about Arizona. At Wickenburg her ink brightens: *Seems good to see somebody we know*. The Prescotts were good to us, good for us. I wish I could do better justice of recollection to Winnie, who was as approximate to me then as in memory: a ranch duchess who did not quite know how to connect with children. I remember only that she would stroll from room to room in their Battle Creek ranch house with her coffee cup in hand as if taking it for a walk. But Allen I can see as if he has been next door these past forty-eight years. Round in the shoulder and middle, squarish of jaw and nose, he resembled a droll upright turtle. Where my father went at ranch tasks in a compelled flurry, Allen entertained himself with them; he thought up a name for every cow

49

he had and spent the time to teach each one to come running when summoned. My parents were not predisposed to like ritzy cow-naming neighbors, but Allen and for that matter Winnie were so puckish about their own highfalutin tendencies that they were hard not to be fond of. A bit later there at Wickenburg it must have been a sharp loss for my folks when the companionable Prescotts migrated back north to begin spring on their Battle Creek ranch. But they left us with all they could. It was the Prescotts who gave us the desert.

The cabin in the cactus-patch foothills wasn't ours and it wasn't even theirs; the place belonged to some Wickenburg acquaintance of the Prescotts who charitably let us cubbyhole ourselves there while Dad recuperated.

Not hot and cold water and so on, but more the ranch style—2 rooms, but we are just going to use one, my mother described to Wally the bargain castle in the sand. *The nice part is it costs no rent.*

Fie upon Phoenix, auf Wiedersehen to Alzona Park and specters of escaped Germans. Out there where we at first didn't know joshua from yucca from cholla from ocotillo, the trio of us got up each morning with nothing recognizable around except one another and the weary Ford. Neighbors now consisted of lizards and scorpions. The mountains wavering up from every horizon around Wickenburg looked ashen, dumpy. The highest lump anywhere around was, gruesomely, Vulture Peak. No pelt of sagebrush to soften this country for us, either; saguaro cacti, with their spiky mittens out, stubbled the hills. Where the familiar black-green of Montana's jack-pines would have shadowed, here the bare green blush of paloverde scarcely inflected the gulches—arroyos—and under every other bristling contortion of vegetation, prickly pears crouched like shin-hunting pygmies in ambush. Even the desert birdsounds had a jab to them, the ha *ha* of a Gambel's quail invisibly derisive in the bush, the yap of a Gila woodpecker scolding us from his cactus penthouse.

I loved every fang and dagger of it.

Any bloodline is a carving river and parents are its nearest shores. At the Faulkner Creek ranch I had learned to try out my mother's limits by running as fast as I could down the sharp shale slope of the ridge next to the ranch house. How I ever found it out without cartwheeling myself to multiple fractures is a mystery, but the avalanche angle of that slope was precisely as much plunge as I could handle as a headlong four- and five-year-old. The first time my visiting grandmother saw one of my races with the law of gravity, she refused ever to watch again. Even my father, with his survivor's-eye view from all the times life had banged him up, even he was given pause by those vertical dashes of mine, tyke roaring drunk on momentum. But my mother let me risk. Watched out her kitchen window my every wild down-hiller, hugged herself to bruises while doing so, but let me. Because she knew something of what was ahead? Can it have been that clear to her, that reasoned? The way I would grow up, after, was contained in those freefall moments down that shale-bladed slope. In such plunge, if you use your ricochets right, you steal a kind of balance for yourself; you make equilibrium moment by moment because you have to. Amid the people and places I was to live with, I practiced that bouncing equilibrium and carried it on into a life of writing, freefalling through the language. My father's turn at seeing me toward gravitational independence would come. But my mother's came first and it came early, in her determination that I should fly free of the close coddling she'd had as an ill child. At the Faulkner Creek place she turned me loose in that downhill spree. Here in our second Arizona life, she daily set me free into the cactus jungle.

Where lessons were quick. One pant cuff instantaneously full of fiendish tiny needles and you know not to brush by a prickly pear again.

The saguaros seemed to welcome me into the desert democracy of light. Morning shadows of several-armed cactus in stretching dance toward Wickenburg, stubby clumps at noon, reversed elongation toward the Hieroglyphic Mountains in honor of evening. Here even I, according to the shadow possibilities of my prowling boy-body and its swoopbrimmed hat, was a hive of wizards.

And so did the Ford play into my newest seizure of imagination, its exaggerated groundcloud of shade the perfect pantomime companion for the game of Allen-Prescott-and-the-runaway-Terraplane. Allen told it on himself, how his Hudson Terraplane—an old behemoth sedan he had cut the back out of, hybridizing it into a kind of deluxe ranch runabout and carryall—hung up on a low shale bank when he was puttering out to fix fence between his ranch and Faulkner Creek. When he got behind the car with a crowbar, his mighty pry liberated the Terraplane but also flung him to his knees. By the time he could clamber back onto his feet the car was trundling away at a surprising pace. That tale of the Terraplane planing across the terra, Allen in hotfoot pursuit, was tailormade for a lone boy and a suggestible Ford, you just bet it was. In and out of the parked coupe I flung myself, its shadowline and mine the pageant of Allen's frantic chase, a pretend reel of barbwire bucking out and bowling wickedly at his/my shins, mock fence-posts clacketing against each other as they fly out of the bed of the bounding runaway, reenacted dodging of a five-pound nailbox tipping over, the Terraplane/Ford laying a silver trail of spikes.

The desert, it is said, makes people more absolute. While I kite around among the cacti, my father pegs away at the chore of recuperation, and the indigo of the desert night draws down into my mother's pen.

Everyone else is in bed but I'm not ready to go just yet, so will spend my time writing you. Pretty chilly tonight. Keeps me busy poking wood in the fire. . . .

We are all pretty well at present. Charlie is getting along alright or seems to be, anyway. His side is sore yet, and he has to be careful, but that is to be expected. . . .

This is a good place to rest, & that's what Charlie needs. . . . I always thought a desert is just nothing, but have changed my mind. . . . It is really beautiful here, in the desert way. . . .

Got 2 welcome letters from you yesterday. So glad to hear from you, Wally, and know you're O.K. Was surely too bad about your buddy being lost in that storm. I don't think any of us have a good idea of what you guys have to go through.

* * *

Logbook of the *Ault*, March 19, 1945, off Okinawa:
0814 SIGHTED ENEMY PLANE (JUDY) MAKING SUICIDE
DIVE ON FORMATION. PLANE WAS TAKEN UNDER FIRE
AND SHOT DOWN BY A.A. FIRE. PLANE FELL OFF PORT
BEAM OF USS *ESSEX*. . . . OBSERVED USS *FRANKLIN* AND
USS *WASP* BURNING AT A DISTANCE.

1318 SIGHTED TWO ENEMY PLANES (ZEKES) MAKING
ATTACK ON FORMATION. MANEUVERED AT EMERGENCY
TURNS AND SPEEDS. COMBAT AIR PATROL SHOT DOWN
ONE DISTANT 5 MILES. OTHER PLANE MADE SUICIDE
DIVE ON TASK GROUP AND WAS SHOT DOWN BY ANTIAIR-
CRAFT FIRE.

2145 . . . COVERING THE WITHDRAWAL OF USS
FRANKLIN, BADLY DAMAGED AND IN TOW TO WEST-
WARD.

March, 1991. I am in Wickenburg again, to write
this of us. Now as then, a war is on; this time, American
planes are bombing the boots off the Iraqis. Yellow rib-
bons of hasty patriotism blossom on every streetlight,
flagpole, porchpost, in contrast to 1945's here and there
glimpses of windows showing gold stars of the war dead.

Compared with Phoenix where an Americanism of
another kind, an arterial slum of the dark and poor and
addicted, has consumed the Alzona Park housing project
without a trace, this town as my mother and father and
I met it in World War Two is surprisingly enterable
again. Wickenburg then was still mostly burg, with the

fancy houses and subdivisions only starting to be poked onto the hills around, but then as now the place banked on the one commodity it knew it had: sun. Basking beside the Hassayampa River composing sonnets for itself—"the wine that is called air" was one trill tried out by the weekly paper while we were there—Wickenburg was likably frank about what it was up to. You didn't need to be the reincarnation of Marco Polo to recognize that the accommodations along the main street, Wickenburg Way, were there to sieve tourists through, while around the corner along Tegner Street ordinary town life was carried on. Guest ranches were a sideline Wickenburg quickly tumbled to; in a historical blink, Indian territory had given way to Dudeland. Signs for trail rides and chuckwagon dining notwithstanding, my parents must have only ever semi-believed that there existed a class of people willing to pay to mimic, for a few tenderbottom hours at a time, the horseback mode that had governed life at Moss Agate and the Doig homestead and Faulkner Creek.

Requiem for the lariat proletariat. Even then the pools of us were drying up, and we never were many. Maybe cryogenic moments of my parents' existence, museum instances of how she sat small but vivid in the saddle beneath a mountain arch of stone and how he gallantly performed in cattle corral and bronc arena, are the only currency by which Berneta and Charlie Doig mean anything to today's world. But coming again to Wickenburg, I find the inscribing shadows of the desert saying much more of them.

*　　*　　*

In the cabin of then, my father is mending from his surgery day by day. He is also growing jumpy, as he tends to do when he doesn't have work in his hands.

We have stuck to cabin routine, except when Dad reports in to the Wickenburg doctor once a week. A Sunday ago, Allen Prescott drove out to say good-bye before their trip home to Montana, so it is Allen who was behind the camera, catching a bit of his own shadow on the side of the cabin, for the only Arizona picture of my mother and father and me together. Dad and I with our workaday hats on (his with that jaunty crimp, mine sitting on me flatbrimmed as a lampshade) while my mother, wearing a striped frock and high heels and with her hair fixed, looks like the one doing the Sunday visiting to this bareboard abode.

Here it is Sun. again, our first visitless week. But even in this pottery landscape we are not as alone as we'd assumed. Regular as breakfast, desert cattle like bony Moss Agate cow ghosts plod past the cabin. My parents keep trying to figure out how many acres, how many *miles*, of the Sonora each gaunt beef has to range across in a day; the things look like they'd eat the eyebrows off you.

My father and I are on the hoof ourselves each desert dusk. While my mother clears away the supper dishes, he and I take his prescribed daily walk. "That doc's favorite medicine is shoe leather," my father has said more than once.

Ever since Dad came out of the hospital I have stayed as close to him as a sidecar, because you never know. Now out we go as always along the road to the foot of the big hill and back, far enough to be dutiful without getting silly about it. Cactus garden to the right of us, to the left of us. Wicks of thorn stand especially sharp in the evening desert light, every saguaro spacing itself prudently away from its neighbors' prickles, all the ocotillos in surprise binge of leaves between their devilwhip barbs. The last of sunlight retreats from us up the foothills and then the ashy mountainslopes. The mountains I have understood to be the Higherglyphics, because obviously they are higher.

"It's going to be a chilly one tonight," my father tastes from the air, and I swear I begin to notice the cool as he is saying it. The feel of existence seems different here from the huge weathers of Montana, the desert temperature instead registering itself degree by degree as if coats of my skin were constantly being added by day and subtracted by evening.

This evening we have barely turned around to start home to the cabin before the wind comes up, strong as soon as it arrives. Around us the entire desert gallops in the sudden blow, the tops of creosote bushes wobbling, the stiff paloverde and mesquite abruptly restless, dust haze mounting into the air between us and the mountains. Everything up and running except the trudging us. For the first time in my life I can walk as fast as my plunge-ahead father, slowed as he is by the incised soreness in his side.

"Wouldn't this just frost your ass," my father mutters as we hang on to our hats, although the wind doesn't seem to me *that* chilly.

Falling night, the swooping wind, whatever is on my father's mind, all propel us rapidly into the cabin. My mother is not alone.

"Look who I found," she says in a loving tone.

The visitor skeptically sizes up my father and me to see whether we constitute fit company for the likes of himself and my mother, and at last gives us a medium welcome by licking his own nose.

There is a little white slickhaired dog strayed in here today, an old dog, hasn't been too well fed.

"More like, who found you," my father says in his driest manner. In his stockman life, dogs had been a natural necessity. Cowdogs, sheepdogs, dogs that were merely dogs and barely even that, the Faulkner Creek ranch had boiled with dogs. So my father got along fine with dogs in their place, which was anywhere but in the house. Or as he had to put it constantly in his years with my mother, not-in-the-damn-house.

Of course I let him in and fed him, you know me.

No neutrals among us, but I was closest. From the time I was big enough to toddle I possessed a dog of my own, a perfect German shepherd pup who grew up to be a kind of furry gendarme assigned to me as I caromed around next to Faulkner Creek. Pup had lasted until the summer before we embarked to Arizona, when we were living temporarily in White Sulphur Springs. The town had a dog poisoner, some strychninic fiend, and after Pup died in crawling agony before our eyes I was never the same about dogs again. Now I edge up and put in a minority share of petting, but this desert mutt is no Pup.

My father is on that same theme, pointing out that this specimen amounts to more mooch than pooch. My mother, though, is all but pedigreeing her guest on the spot.

"There you go, yes," as she scratches his mangy ears,

"you just want to be petted and petted, don't you," fully doing so.

"Berneta," my father takes his stand. "You're not having that dog with us. We don't need a dog in Arizona."

"I know," says my mother as if she doesn't know any such thing. "But it's cold out there on that old desert tonight, isn't it, Mooch? Here, up on the chair, up, Mooch." Professional tramp that he is, the mutt obligingly scrabbles onto the seat of a straightback chair and sits with his head turned toward my mother, who immediately pays off in cookies.

"He gets put back out in the morning," my father tries another declaration. "For good."

The dog looks at my father, gives a sniff, then arranges himself on the chair for a nap. My mother laughs and gets out her letter paper while my father and I settle at the other end of the kitchen table for our other routine of his recuperation. He and I are using his enforced leisure on a jigsaw puzzle of the Grand Canyon, yielded up by the cabin. (*Big one, 500 pieces*, my mother records appropriately into the letter. She wisely holds back on helping us except when a piece is so obvious she just can't resist.) Naturally we saw the actual colossus of canyon on our journey from Montana and were properly astonished that the Colorado River, responsible for it all, amounted to a mere brown string of water off in the distance. But whether our own assembling of the Grand Canyon is ever going to catch up with the Colorado's is an open question. The canyon's show of colors, layered as rainbows, lies like chopped-up crayons all over our half of the table. This five-year-old me has the unholy patience of a glacier, which means that my father must contend not only with half a thousand puzzle pieces but with my method of torturously trying them one after another in a single amoebic opening. Also, I keep wanting to know how this piece or that looks in terms of his colorblindness—"But Daddy, what color do you *think* it looks like?"

My father chews his lip a lot during our innings at the jigsaw, but he is determined we are going to finish the damned puzzle or know-the-reason-why.

The dog suddenly wakes up, sits up blinking at us as if indignant at the excessive noise of puzzle pieces being moved. My mother puts down her pen and gives his ears a restorative scratching.

My father has been eyeing the dog as if pretty sure its next trick will be to pick our pockets. But now Dad cocks his head toward the kitchen wall. "Listen a bit, everybody."

Grutch.

The three of us and the dog listen, all right, the very knots in the wall seem to listen.

Grutch grutch.

The sound keeps stopping, then furtively *grutch*ing again. A scraping on the desert gravel, whatever this is. Working at—digging under the cabin?

By now my father knows in alarm what—who—this invasion is. And as quick as he knows, my mother and I know. Prisoners of war! More of those German submariners who tunneled out of the Papago Park camp through caliche that the U.S. Army figured was encasing them like vault steel. The SOBs were regular Teutonic badgers.

My father rises out of his chair into whispered action.

"Berneta, get in the other room with Ivan and that—"
The dog is already gone, scooted under the bed.

"No," my mother whispers back with utter firmness.
"I'm coming with." The time in the Sixteen country
when my father tangled with a bear that was marauding
nightly into the sheep, he looked up after having thrust
the rifle in the bear's ribs for a desperate fatal shot and
found my mother standing on the cutbank just above
him, holding a lantern, watching the whole show. Now
again, for better or worse, she is adding her ninety-five
pounds against the submariners of the desert.

"Ivan, then, go in the other room," my father directs.

"But I want to fight the Ger—"

"I-tell-ye, get-in-that-other-room!"

I compromise as far as the doorway to the other room.
My father grimly scans the cabin walls, trying to conjure
a gunrack and .30–06 rifle out of bare board. *GRUTCH*,
the in-tunneling all but grinds up through the floor.

My father grabs the only weapon at hand, which is
the broom, and eases to the door, my mother closer
behind him than his shadow.

In the lantern light the lone attacker blinks, as startled
to see my father and mother as they are by its incursion.

Then the wandering cow gives a moo and a chew, and
goes back to gobbling the potato peelings my mother had
dumped in the garbage box, skidding the box bottom
across the desert floor with another *grutch*.

My mother and father ribbed each other for days about
the cow showdown. Cabin life seemed ready to blossom
along with the desert.

We have learned to like Arizona, so far as the country is concerned, my mother at last is able to tell Wally. Probably not coincidentally, her report on my father is also sunny.

Charlie is improving every day. I do so hope he can feel good now.

Meanwhile the issue of the slickhaired dog took care of itself; the next morning after breakfast, the itinerant pooch demanded to be let out and kept on going.

I still am scooting back and forth from the cabin to the cactus shadow show, fired by my latest chapter of imagination.

Ivan is busy looking for gold. Every rock he picks up he asks Charlie if it is gold.

Then the weather turned. That last of winter, late March of 1945, Wickenburg as the world's toasty oasis all of a sudden lacked the element of sunshine. Oh yes, the rains were tinting up the valley of the Hassayampa in rare fashion, as a matter of fact the lushest year since before the war. *Everything so green,* my mother's pen granted. It wasn't just our outlander imaginations that the saguaro cacti looked more portly every day; they indeed were fattening on the rain, the precious moisture cameled up inside their accordion-style inner works. But gauge it as you will, such a spate of precipitation still amounts to, well, rainy days. The *Wickenburg Sun,* trying weekly to convince us its masthead name wasn't a fib, resorted to running the words of a faithful annual visitor who claimed that as chilly and rainy as this season was, he still would not trade the north half of Maricopa County (i.e., Phoenix pointedly excluded) for the whole blooming state of California.

Plainly this desert climate was a more complicated proposition than we had thought. My mother and father started working at the weather in earnest, telling each other that a little cloud cover now maybe was no bad thing, shade in the bank, so to speak, for they'd also been hearing about the local summer temperatures that would by-God-bake-your-eyeballs. Cross that stovetop if and when we came to it, they took turns maintaining, and in the meantime maybe a little cloud cover . . .

Then they woke up one morning to the desert under snow.

Sure been having the weather, my mother jabbed onto paper to Wally. *Make you think you're in Montana.*

Make you think your mental compass needle was off course for more than just that day, in fact. The snow vanished as spectrally as it arrived, but the climate we sought here stayed elusive, chill and rain in its place. My father couldn't take life easy too much longer, particularly in this uneasy desert spring, and nights now, he and my mother talk things over. The possibly not too distant end of the war. The way Arizona is sorting itself out to them and isn't. Hammers are in song in Wickenburg as they were in Phoenix, the subdividing of Arizona an idea that has occurred to every boomer at once. But what are the prospects for people such as us? Wickenburg aside, there did exist a ranching Arizona too, where they grew something besides blisters on dudes. My father had his eye on the comfortably western town of Prescott—favorably named—in the veldtlike cattle country across the Hieroglyphic Mountains. The Grand Canyon puzzle more and more becomes my own enterprise as the two of them put up their pieces of "*I wonder if"* and *"What we maybe ought to"* into the air of our future.

Quite a gabfest, my mother puts down in her desert chronicle to Wally and ultimately to me, and I am surprised when I find she doesn't even remotely mean hers and my father's. *The old miner did all the talking, just about*.

But yes, the miner. Guerrilla cattle aside, our only caller at the cabin.

Before realizing dudes and tourists were the real lode, Wickenburg originated as a goldstrike town, and prospectors still were tramping around in the hills trying to hit the yellow rainbow again. I dream our miner upward from his visit to my mother's recording pen on the twenty-second day of March, 1945. Story-become-person, he comes refusing to look like a desert oreseeker is expected to, other than a few missing finger joints. Instead of shag and beard he sports a precise white mustache like a sharp little awning over his mouth, and a snowy pompadour he keeps in place by lifting his hat straight up when he takes it off in highly reluctant acknowledgment of my mother, womankind. Or maybe he is simply uncorking everything stored up since he last kept company with anyone besides himself in his shaving mirror.

In windjammer style he fast sets us straight about the war (England is who we ought to be fighting) and about the president (Franklin The-Hell-No Roosevelt, in the miner's indignant rendition of the person who took the nation off the gold standard).

Wide-eyed I wait for the battle to erupt over President Roosevelt, great voice that strode out of the radio with every word wearing epaulettes, president for perpetuity if the votes of my parents have anything to do with it.

But skirmish is all anybody wants to risk here, my mother saying only that at least people don't need to eat gophers anymore as they did during Hoover's Depression and my father saying at least Roosevelt is aware of the existence of the working man and the miner saying that when you come right down to it England and Roosevelt are only pretty much the same blamed thing, you can hear it in how they both talk.

Politics disposed of, the miner plunges on to his experiences in the desert generally and here in the Wickenburg country in particular, which is what my folks want to hear from him, local knowledge. Arizoniana, not to mention Wickenburg weather wisdom, they could stand to have by the bale. Used to dealing with loopy sheepherders, my father and mother cross their arms and let the soliloquist unravel while I restlessly wish he'd get going on how to tell gold from rock.

Then one particular squirm of mine seems to remind our filibustering guest of something. Montana he is unacquainted with, he announces, but he has been to Dakota, practically the same.

"I was about the size of your fellow here," he indicates me, then squints as if making a vital adjustment. "Little bigger. Anyways, both my own folks had passed away with mountain fever and so my uncle tucked me into his family. This was when he was running a freight outfit into Deadwood, Dakota, the kind of mule train they called 'eight eights.' Eight teams of eight mules each, three wagons—no, I'm lying again—*two* wagons to each mule team. This one day my uncle hustled home and got us all, my aunt and his own kids and me, and said we better come downtown and see this. So we went down and here was a big freight jam, right in that one long street of Deadwood. What's happened was, all these freight outfits had lit in from Fort Pierre and Bismarck on one side of the gulch and from Cheyenne and those places on the other, and now couldn't none of them get out either way, frontwards or back. There was teams there of just all descriptions, eight-yoke ox teams pulling three wagons, little outfits with two horses or four horses, mostly mule teams like my uncle's on the Cheyenne end of the traffic. Everything jammed up so tight for about a mile, you could have run a dog on the backs of those freight teams from one end of Deadwood to the other. Everybody's standing around saying 'This is no good,' and finally the big freighters got together and talked it over. One man in the bunch made a motion to appoint my uncle the captain of straightening this thing out. My uncle said, 'Well, boys, if you want me to, I'll take charge.' They said, 'We want you to take charge. Whatever you say is law and we'll back you.' My uncle said, 'Let's get a little more backing than that,' and he went over to his lead wagon and come back with two six-shooters in his belt. So him and the rest of the bunch started through town looking over the mess and my uncle said, 'We might as well start right here,' and he started them in on moving the little outfits to the sidestreets by hand. The little rigs of two horses, four horses, they put them up alleys and onto porches and just anywhere they could find, and that way they'd get some room to bend out a big ox or mule team. It took my uncle and them all night and into the next morning, sorting all those outfits out. He did something in getting that jam cleared, my uncle did."

Magical uncles. Out there ropewalking the dream latitudes, Deadwood, Okinawa, sorting oxen and mules by hand, preserving the *Ault* from submarines below and dive-bombers above. Uncle Sam even, in the cartoons kicking the behinds of Hitler and Tojo. Whatever marvel needed doing, uncles were the key. Wait a minute, though. Wasn't this mustache-talker awful old to be in on knowledge about uncles? It was a new thought, that uncles were available to just anybody.

Abruptly the miner declares he has to skedaddle back to his claim, as if needing to collect the nuggets it's laid that afternoon. Dad and I walk with him to the road while my bemused mother makes a start on supper.

Still talking a streak, out of nowhere the miner breaks in on himself and asks what brings us to Arizona.

Dad could answer this in his sleep. "My wife's health—"

"Figured so. Could hear it in her." The miner knocks on his own chest. "Got a chuteful of rocks, don't she, there in her lungs. She's young to have it like that."

My father looks as though he has been hit from a blind side. To him, my mother's breathing is not nearly the alarming wheezes of her Montana seizures, or for that matter of our first harrowing night in Arizona four months ago. North of here in the auto court at the town of Williams, high up on the Coconino Plateau, she had put in a horrendous night of gasping spasms. My father would swear on a stack of Bibles that she had improved every foot of the way down from nightmarish Williams to this desert floor. True, one other severe spell hit her during our Phoenix try, but not nearly as bad as that Williams siege, as any of a dozen heart-hammering emergency runs from the Faulkner Creek ranch. Surely to God this desert air is making Berneta better, isn't it? Yet how much better, if an utter stranger can pick out the trouble in her lungs as casually as the tumult in a seashell.

My father stares at the miner. Finally he can say only: "She's . . . thirty-one."

WHITE SULPHUR SPRINGS
APRIL
16
1945
MONT.

Dear Wally—
Winona and I spent Saturday making
formals and catching mice.

I can hear that day of mice and thread.

The needle of Winona's portable sewing machine sings over the material to the treadlebeat of her foot, our kitchen table is gowned with the chiffon she is coaxing to behave into hem. This way and that and the other, she jigsaws the pattern pieces she and my mother have scissored out. My mother is no bigger than a minute in build and Winona minuter yet, so they are resorting to a lot in these prom dresses. The latest nomination has been ruffles.

"I think ruffles would go okay, Nonie, don't you? Give us a little something to sashay?"

"What the hey, we'll ruffle a bunch up and see," pronounces Winona. Her voice is bigger than she is, deep, next thing to gruff. "If I can find my cussed ruffler." The sewing machine treadle halts while Winona conducts a clinking search through her attachments box. "Did you have the radio on, Berneta, the other day? I didn't know a thing about it until the kiddos told me the next morning. I about dropped my teeth."

"I wish to Halifax I hadn't heard, but I did. I had it on while I was in here trying to scrub down that old—"

Where I am holed up behind the couch in the living room, as usual overhearing for all I am worth, comes the somersault snap of another mousetrap going off.

"My turn at the little devils?" Winona volunteers.

"I'll fling this one," says my mother, "you're doing so good on the dresses."

"I thought Ringling has mice something fierce," Winona gives out with. "But cripes, this place!"

"We tried a cat, did I tell you?" An old marmalade stray one, half its tail gone, whom my mother nonetheless cooed *kitten-katten* to. "He only lasted two days. Charlie swears the mice ran the cat out of town."

Both women laugh, until I hear my mother putting on overshoes to take the expired mouse out to the garbage barrel, feel the wind make its presence all through the house when she opens the back door. Blowy April, a thousand and fifty miles north of our Arizona try. We have reverted to Montana, pulling out of Wickenburg at the end of March (*Kind of anxious to get home, see everybody, find out how I'm going to feel, figure out what we are going to do this summer*, my mother's last words to Wally from the desert cabin) to climb back up the continent through Flagstaff and Kanab and Provo and Salt Lake City and Pocatello and Dillon and Twin Bridges— and after all that, we still are nowhere much. This rented house on a side street in White Sulphur Springs is as dreary as it is drafty, its only companionable feature the mob of mice.

Busy busy busy, Winona's Singer goes again. I laze in my own territory, the triangle cave of couchback and room corner it angles across. My books, my trucks, my tubby *Ault*, are cached in here with me out of the prevailing weather. The wind steadily tries to pry out the nearest windowpane. *Seems as though it blows & storms all the time*, my mother has reported this polar Montana spring to Wally, *we're having our March weather in April*. We are having gabstorms and earquakes, if I know anything about it. Since Thursday I've nearly listened myself inside out. This is a job with work to it, this spying on history. Who can tell what will distill next out of the actual air, after Thursday afternoon when my mother had her programs on, *Ma Perkins* or some such, I wasn't much listening until the news voice cut in: "We interrupt this program to bring you a special bulletin . . ."

When the bulletin was over, I came out from behind the couch on all fours, then stood up curious into another age.

In the kitchen, stock-still, scrubbing brush still in her hand where she had been slaving away at the rust stains on the ancient sink drainboard, my mother stood staring at the radio as though trying to see the words just said.

"Mama? When Daddy gets home, are we going to wash the car in the creek?"

"I . . . I don't think so, dear. President Roosevelt's funeral isn't going to be here."

Everything rattles on in the kitchen now, full days later; the dressmaking, the chitchat, their medical opinions on my father who, sore side or not, goes winging out of the house every day to put in twelve hours in a lambing shed (*he really shouldn't be working but then you know Charlie*), rosters of who's home on leave from the war and apt to be met up with at the prom (the White Sulphur Springs high school spring formal amounts to a community dance, as any dance in that lonely Big Belt–edged country tends to), denunciations of this wintry spring, you name it and the smart cookies in the kitchen will do you a two-woman chorus of it. This peppy visit from Winona amounts to a special bulletin itself. Cute yet industrious, Winona looks like a half-pint version of Rosie the Riveter except that, slang and gravelly in-this-for-the-duration voice and all, she is a schoolteacher. Winona I suppose I am a bit shy of, her firecracker energy, her sassy eyes. Kiddo, she calls me. But really, *kiddo* is a hundred times better than the excruciating *Pinky* which some of White Sulphur's downtown denizens call me because of my red mop of hair, and in the right tone of voice I think it also makes an improvement over *Ivan*.

Now Winona is off on hats. She's seen a zippy spring number in the Monkey Ward catalogue she is sure she could make for my mother. Living out of suitcases as we have been for the past half year my mother's wardrobe can stand any first aid it can get, so the women talk headgear until the next mousetrap springs. This time Winona, insisting she wouldn't want to get out of practice, takes a turn at disposing of the deceased mouse. Quick as she scoots back in from the garbage barrel, the conversation again becomes fabric and color and whether to veil or not, yet how much more than hat chat is going on.

Wally, you asked me my opinion of you and Winona.

"Going together" was the description for Wally and Winona, fine fudge of a phrase. Did it mean merely fooling around with one another while the good time lasted or drawing toward each other into inevitable destiny of matrimony? Evitable or in, that is the question for Wally out there on the *Ault* with an ocean of time to think. He has put in about a thousand days in the navy by now, and Winona even more in the teacherage at Ringling, and across such a space of young life maybe a sag sets in. Her V-mail to him stays bright and kidding, but as she points out, there is only so much of yourself you can provide in 25 words or so.

Nonie has a good education . . .

Tricky duty for Berneta's pen here. Close chum to Winona, but also Wally's older and married sister being asked for advice.

My mother ends up doing them a tick-tack-toe for going beyond going together.

. . . is a good cook, a fair housekeeper, and a real seamstress as well as a good sport. She has her faults, so do we all. But I think she is the kind that if she loves a guy she'll stick with him through Hell & high water. So if you think you two can make a go of life together I'm certainly for you. But it is up to you to know what you feel in your heart.

Now she pauses over the factor that has winked between Wally and Winona since their first moment and is neither X nor O.

There is a few years difference in your age . . .

Quite the picture of a strapping young beau, the prewar Wally amounted to. Abundant black teenage hair in the long-may-it-wave 1940s style; that ever likable face, ready for anything; muscular frame you could pick out clear across town when the town happened to be Ringling.

Decades later when he had become royally bellied, amid one of our trout excursions I came up on him dabbling over his tackle box as he sweetly crooned, "I just want a Paper Doll, to call my own . . . but those flirty-flirty guys, with their flirty-flirty eyes . . ."

Which way the flirting originally ran between Wally and Winona would be instructive to know, as it would clarify whose waiting out the war was the more serious:

the durational teacher holding the fort at the Ringling schoolhouse or the shipboard combatant seven years younger than she.

. . . but I can't see where that should make much difference. It hasn't in my marriage, I know, and there are more years difference between us than there are you kids. If a couple loves one another enough they can overcome most anything that happens to come along.

Those four words were the only ones my mother underlined, ever, in her entire set of letters to Wally.

September 6, 1990. Winona sits at the table in the double-wide mobile home, thirty-five atrocious miles from the nearest paved road. Her face is beyond wrinkled, riveted, but her eyes still are glamour girl. I flinch at her chronic ripping cough, brutal echo of my mother's lungs. I, though, must be even more alarming to Winona: freckleface redheaded kiddo of forty-plus years ago now silvering like a tree snag. If my mother's face or Wally's reside anywhere beneath the gray storm-mask of beard on me, Winona can't seem to find them.

Nonetheless I have been coffeed, fed, welcomed in out of a past, half a Montana away, where so much happened and just as much didn't. Whichever of them first tapered the enthusiasm for going together by V-mail, Wally and Winona were over with before World War Two was. Not long after, she traded in schoolteaching for a return to this—a remote, almost reckless reach of land which had been her parents', homesteaded by them, clung to somehow through the Depression, through any number of years even more arid than usual in this dry heart of the state. Winona has been married, "since coming home," to a wiry ranchman who patiently installed twelve miles of pipe to furnish reliable water to their cattle. Evidently a matched set in all ways, Winona and her husband both are pared down to life in this short-grass country, not a gram of excess on them or their ground. I figured I had seen every kind of Montana endurance, but the ranching done here by this weatherstropped pair, now into their seventies, is very nearly Australian-outback in its austerity, a scant herd of cattle specked across twenty entire miles of rangeland. "It's all like this," Winona's husband gives up-and-down motions of his hand to show how their land stands on end in a welter of abrupt buttes and clay cliffs. Their mobile home he catskinned in by tractor, no trailer-truck able to fit around the hairpin curves of the dirt track into here.

From here Ringling seems as distant as Agincourt, but Wally even yet is a chancy topic for Winona. After the war, which is to say after they had gone separate paths to the altar, she met up with him only once, at a rodeo. Neither of them, she tells me carefully, had much to say to the other. Bare word did reach her of his death; but until now she has not heard of his second and third marriages, two wives out of three at his funeral.

After a long moment she says in a voice dry as dust: "Nice to be so loved."

Winona speaks more gladly of my mother and my father. She remembers regularly mailing cartons of cigarettes to Arizona for my father that war-rationed winter. My mother she paints without surprise as "a real good conversationalist"—then Winona breaks into another terrible coughing spasm, terribly reminiscent. When her breath returns, Winona suddenly switches memory to me when I was a tyke falling in love with words: "You knew a lot of things. I remember you going through your books, telling me all the things in them."

Smoke interrupts the afternoon. Winona's husband catches the whiff first, she about one sniff later. I still don't, having inherited the useless Ringer nose—substantial in every way except the capacity to smell—but when they pile out of the mobile home and start scanning upwind, I certainly do, too. A prairie fire would burn through this country until the moon was cooked. So I am relieved when Winona and her husband categorize the smoke as general, a haze from far-off forest fires.

Unincinerated one more time, the ranch couple take it for granted that I'll follow back inside for further gab and caffeine, although I tag behind to keep peering around at this backland enterprise of theirs. In one direction the giant bald ridge which the road kinks down from, in two others sharp slopes eroded at the top into chopped-up formations of pale ashen clay, and for a finale the distant river badlands which aren't much worse than any other of the country crumpled all around here. Every horizon ruptured and stark. Liver-Eating Johnson supposedly lurched through this neck of the weeds, hunting Indians like they were partridges, in the previous mad century. Since then, this stretch of land has been occupied by people willing to give it the benefit of the doubt for forty or fifty years at a time. I struggle to imagine Wally here, superimpose him as the husband coping with this dryland dowry, so far away from his fishing holes and elk meadows. Never.

* * *

Back in the kitchen arsenal of 1945, my mother and Winona wage on against chiffon, mice, life and fate and budget.

"Before I forget. How much did the material set us back?"

"All of $4.63."

"Then your time. Nonie, I have to give you something for all your sewing."

"Like fun you will. You came all the way to Ringling and got me, so you're out the cost of your gas, let's just—"

"No, now, that's not the same as—" Another mortal whack of a mousetrap cuts off both voices.

"Hit 'im again, McGinty!" Winona whoops. "Berneta, how in the world many is that, just since noon?"

"Twelve, this'll make. Keeps a person busy just keeping count." This must be the trap in the grocery cupboard, from the sound of my mother's voice going enclosed. "How many more jillion dozen do you suppose—" Then she exclaims: "Nonie, talk about mouse trappers, we're it! Ivan! Come see!"

Already I am out of my couch cave, scrambling in from the living room. A lilac cloud of chiffon smothers half the kitchen, but over at the cupboard Winona is on tiptoe beside my mother peering in at their catch. I hop up on a chair to see.

Double bull's-eye! *Two* dead mice in *one* trap, clamped neck to neck in their permanent race for the bait of cheese.

The victorious trappers are already at the next stage,

how to hang on to credit for their feat. "Charlie will never believe we're in here catching them two at a time."

"I know what. We'll just save the trap for him the way it is, for proof."

Winona and my mother ruthlessly giggle.

What can account for my mother's high spirits at being back in that drafty mousy attic of Montana, the mile-up-and-then-some Big Belt country where sour winter stayed on past the spring dance?

I have stared holes into those mountains, those sage-scruffed flats and bald Sixteen hills, trying to savvy their hold on her and thus on us, particularly there in severe 1945. The village of Ringling, its railroad future already behind it, was waning into whatever is less than a village. The town of White Sulphur Springs had been handled roughly by the Depression and the war, sagging ever farther from its original dream of becoming a thermal-spring resort. Out around the Smith River Valley, the big ownerships still owned. Moss Agate was being borne down by time to that sole leaning barn of today. All the members of the Ringer family besides my mother were struggling with the armed forces of Japan or with themselves. My father's arena, the Doig homestead and the Wall Mountain rangeland, had fallen from family hands long ago. Looked at clinically, there was not much to come back to, after half a century of Doigs and Ringers hurling themselves at those hills.

But earth and heart don't have much of a membrane between them. Sometimes decided on grounds as elusive as that single transposable *h*, this matter of siting ourselves. Of a place mysteriously insisting itself into us. The saying in our family for possessing plenty of something was that we had oceans of it, and in her final report from the desert to her silent listener on the *Ault*, my mother provided oceans of reasons why we were struggling back north to precisely what we had abandoned. One adios to Arizona she spoke was economic. *So few possibilities for people with a limited supply of money like ourselves to get anywhere in any kind of business.* She saw corporate Phoenix and landvending Wickenburg plain: *It might be better after the war but I think it will be worse.* And the contours of community were beckoning us. *We don't just like the idea of being way down here and all our folks in Montana.* Valid enough in itself, that need for people and places, friends and family, with well-trodden routes of behavior; home is where, when you gossip there, any hearer knows the who what why.

Yet, yet . . . there was unwordable territory, too, in our return to what my mother's letters as early as Phoenix began to mention as *home*. Refusal to become new atomized Americans, Sun Belt suburbanites, and instead going back to Montana's season-cogged life is one thing. Going back specifically to the roughcut Big Belts, the snakey Sixteen country, the Smith River Valley where we Doigs and Ringers could never quite dodge our own dust, all that is quite another. My parents can only have made such a choice from their bottommost natures, moods deep and inscrutable as the keels of icebergs.

Ivan and I were over to see Mom.
My grandmother could hmpf like a member of roy-

alty. She is hmpfing in a major way to my mother, although not *at* my mother; Grandma's range of fire simply tends to take in the entire vicinity.

"At least I got letters from you, dear. I haven't heard from Wallace and Paul in ages, darn their hides."

Like her, I can't imagine why a mere war keeps them from writing. Here I am at not quite six, same age as the war, and already I am matchless on this matter of correspondence. Isn't my Christmas greeting of merry dive-bombers here on Grandma's kitchen wall as though it were by Michelangelo? How natural it comes, hmpfproof artistry, when you are the first grandchild and so far the only.

My mother has been shrewd enough to bring me along handy at her side on this diplomatic mission to her own mother. This is not as supple a scene for her as exterminating with Winona. Our first after-Arizona visit to Grandma carries complications that extend back to the Moss Agate years, where this grayhaired much-done-to woman provided my mother with that peculiar girlhood, threadbare and coddled, and now there's a deal more to come which my mother dreads to have to tell.

Say this for the situation, my grandmother never takes long to sort out to you what's on her mind. Rapidfire, she deems our visit tardy (we have been back from Arizona whole weeks) and assigns the logical reason (my father). She is also snorty that this call of ours is going to be so abbreviated (overnight). Her points made, she proceeds to flood us in fresh-baked cinnamon rolls, oatmeal cookies, and all other kinds of doting.

Between pastry feasts we each furnish Grandma our versions of Arizona. Mine is heavier on cactus than my mother's. Both women are tanking up on coffee, and I am intrigued that Grandma cuts hers with cold water dippered from the sink bucket. I negotiate for a sip—a sipe, Grandma's way of saying it—just to confirm that coffee in this diluted fashion is as awful as it figures to be. It is.

Maybe watered coffee sums up my grandmother's lot. Compared with even my parents, who were not exactly at the head of the caste parade, my grandmother's existence was just this side of the poorhouse. It had been that way from Moss Agate where, with at least a roof over their heads, the Ringers maybe had not been penniless but there were plenty of times when they were dollarless. My grandmother ever after referred to any item that reminded her of Moss Agate as "old junk," which in fact was pretty much what the life there had consisted of— junk cows, a junk ranch. It wouldn't have taken much for society to consider the Ringer family itself junk. True, this grandmother of mine and even my grandfather had fended greatly better as community members than their economics suggested. My grandmother, only a third-grade education to her name, served on the school board so that the Moss Agate country could have a one-room school, and somehow raised the Ringer kids as though their home life wasn't as patchy as it was. My grandfather Tom at least toughed out their marriage until the four children were grown and gone, and brought in whatever he could from second jobs of carpentry and general craftwork. He, I now realize, may have been deviled by a different damage within him than he was ever ascribed; a house painter in his younger life, his mood and health may have fallen prey to the lead used in paint at the time. By whatever shaping, to the end of their separate existences my grandparents, Tom Ringer choring on ranches, Bessie Ringer cooking on ranches, perpetually shifted around under mid-Montana's mountain horizon but could never rise.

Now that she had left him, she has taken shelter here in the Shields River country in another lopsided situation, as cook for a Norwegian widower. Living like nun and monk as far as anybody can tell, the pair of them operate the old Norskie's tidy little outfit, part farm and part cow ranch, here under the long slopes on the west side of the Crazy Mountains. I would bet hard money that the old Norskie never saw fit to break his creamy silence and say so, but the place could not have been run without my indefatigable grandmother: she even did the plowing, with a team of horses. My father or any other veteran ranchman would have shouldered labor like this only on shares. For doing much the same work, and the cooking and housekeeping besides, she eked out a wage from month to month and beyond that she literally had nothing—what we call benefits were nowhere in the picture because even Social Security then was regarded as too great a paperwork burden on owners of farms and ranches, and "agricultural employees" such as my grandmother were specifically excluded from its coverage.

Instead, she had what she was. The only thing about my grandmother that ever went gray was her hair. All else stayed brisk, immutable; the pleasant enough proclamation of face where the origin of my mother's and for that matter mine is instantly read, the body of German sturdiness. The hands and arms of Bessie Ringer were scarred from every kind of barbwire work, yet there she sat hooking away at the most intricate of crochetwork, snowflaking the rough rooms of her existence with doily upon doily. After a schooling that petered out so early, she couldn't much more than handle 1 and 2 for you, but anything you could hum she could sit down to a piano and faithfully play. "The baby is born and his name is Dennis," she would rattle off as her proverb of completing anything, fingerlace or ear-taught tune or the perpetual twice a day milking of cows in that bent-pail life at Moss Agate. There at Moss Agate too, she had been the parent who somewhere always found time to pull on boxing gloves when her sons went through a pugilism phase. And to pamper an asthmatic daughter. Situations she hadn't the foggiest notion of how to handle, she handled. The chicken chapter: softhearted as she was toward all creatures except the human, she could never bear to chop the head off a chicken. Early in her Montana life, when my mother was still a toddler, there came a Sunday when chicken was the only available meal and nobody else was around to do the chopping. My grandmother caught the chicken, tied its legs, put it in the baby buggy with my mother, and trundled down the road a couple of miles to the next ranch to have a neighbor do the neck deed.

Grandma's straight-ahead set of mind came useful for her here in the Norskie situation, too. On no known social scale ought she have been able to fit into the stolid local women's club—merely an itinerant cook, and beyond that, married to somebody she wasn't living with but who definitely was not the Norwegian widower she was under the same roof with—but she impressed those farm wives and ranchwomen with her own stiffbacked rectitude and was brought in. Annually the women drew "secret pal" names out of a hat and each sent whomever they drew little surprise gifts and cards throughout the year. My grandmother undoubtedly was the only peasant plow-woman who was also a secret pal, but she had a saying ready for the way life revealed its surprises, too. "So that's the how of it."

So that was the how of her, my stormfront grandmother. Wide-grained and with hard knots of stubbornness, rilesome and quick to judge and long to hold a grudge. And in the turbulent time to come, I learned to love her for even the magnificence of her shortcomings.

Back there in our visit it is Grandma, you can bet your boots, who comes out with it about my grandfather. Have we seen the old-good-for-nothing?

Dreadfully, we have. Tom Ringer is living in one room of a shanty, the rest of which is used as a chickenhouse. The alfalfa chaff scratched up by the baby chicks *got him down*, my mother has passed the word to Wally from our visit; *one of those short-winded spells . . . a bad one.*

Gnarled and bent as a Knockadoon walking stick, my grandfather; my grandmother, on the other hand, so sturdy she could carry the rest of us over the Crazy Mountains on her back.

My mother, the product of the extremes, tries to give an unflavored report.

"Hmpf," she receives for her trouble. "I just wish to gosh he'd behaved hisself when we were—"

By now I pretty well know where Grandma is going with this, and out I whip to explore the Norskie country.

As ever, Grandma has a panting overfed dog around

like an old lodger. Shep instantly wants to go helling off with me in every direction at once. Him aside, though, this ranch is disappointingly kempt and quiet. No suicide slope for me to roar down as in my Faulkner Creek daredeviltry days. Next I thrash around in vain for the shop, as a blacksmithery is called on a ranch; no alluring rusty nests of iron, no forge with a fanwheel to turn faster and faster into a wondrous straining screech. Nor, can you believe, is there even a bunkhouse, let alone a mussy crew of ranch hands with names like Zoot and Diamond Tony; the Norskie's son from up the creek and the Norskie—and Grandma—handle the calving by themselves.

I have been shortchanged. I know to the snick of his jackknife being opened what my father is doing exactly now, fifty miles north of here in his lambing shed kingdom, jacketing a bum lamb with the hide of a dead one and enforcing the suspicious ewe to adopt the newcomer: "That's right, ye old sister, this is your new one. Get under there, Jakey, and get yourself a meal before she catches on to you." I am missing out on that, for this becalmed mission to Grandma?

Gone goofy with the thrill of having someone to romp with, Shep keeps giving me baths with his old tongue. Dog slobber is limited fun. I evacuate from the ranch yard to the kitchen congress again.

"Sit you down, dear," Grandma welcomes me back to the table as if the sun rises and sets in me, and then their talk buzzes on. At last my mother and her mother have got going on the populace beyond the family. Other people's doings, blessed relief. I nibble the one-more-cookie-but-that's-all which my mother decrees to me while news of this one and that is ruthlessly swapped. So and so is just as much of a scatterbrain as ever and of course thinks she was terribly abused in the service. Had to work a little, something she isn't used to. Thus and such are going to have an increase in the family. Have to feel sorry for any kid with them as parents.

Never more than a sentence away in any of their gossip is the war. The war has consumed Montana. Not in the roaring geared-up military factory fashion of Arizona, but in a kind of mortal evaporation. Young men, and no few women, have been gone for years and in their place the ghostly clink of dogtags from the charnel corners of the world; striplings who have eaten plateloads at the ranch tables of my grandmother and square-danced with my mother and pranced me on a knee are wasting away in prisoner-of-war camps in Germany, have perished in the Bataan death march, been wounded at Palau, fought in the Aleutians and the Marianas and Normandy.

My ears all but turn inside out when Grandma frets to my mother about Wally, where his ship might be, what's happening there in the Pacific. She is mighty right to do so.

Logbook of the *Ault*, May 11, 1945:

1010 SIGHTED ENEMY PLANE (ZEKE) WHICH CAME OUT OF LOW CLOUD ASTERN AND DIVED INTO THE AFTER FLIGHT DECK OF USS *BUNKER HILL*. OBSERVED ANOTHER ENEMY PLANE TO COME FROM ASTERN. OPENED FIRE. PLANE CRASHED INTO *BUNKER HILL* FLIGHT DECK AMIDSHIPS. MANEUVERING AT EMERGENCY TURNS AND SPEEDS. *BUNKER HILL* WAS BURNING FURIOUSLY.

1023 OBSERVED TWO ENEMY PLANES SHOT DOWN IN

DOGFIGHT. A THIRD BEGAN A RUN IN TOWARDS FORMA-
TION AT LOW ALTITUDE WITH A FRIENDLY FIGHTER ON
HIS TAIL. OPENED FIRE WITH ALL GUNS AS PLANE PASSED
STARBOARD QUARTER. . . . PLANE ATTEMPTED TO
MAKE SUICIDE DIVE ON THIS VESSEL AND WAS SHOT
DOWN BY THIS SHIP, FALLING CLOSE ABOARD THE PORT
QUARTER.

And only days ago, the war ate down into my own age
bracket. This had happened a block or so away from us
in White Sulphur, during a collection drive of waste
paper for the war effort. Schoolchildren darting from
house to house, carrying the scrap to the truck, hopping
onto the truckbed to ride to the next houses, the truck
driver thinking everyone was aboard and starting ahead:
crushing under the rear wheels his own seven-year-old
son.

Such a death of a child, even these life-calloused
Ringer women do not talk over. What happened to that
boy has been my interior topic, the imagining of how the
wheels couldn't/wouldn't have made their fatal claim if
it had been me. The not-quite-six-year-old's dream insu-
lation from the world, quite convinced I am deathproof.

Out of nowhere, which is to say everywhere, I
abruptly am hearing:

". . . afraid you'd gone to old Arizona for good," my
grandmother to my mother. My mother back to her,
"Charlie figured—we figured we had to give it a try
there."

Grandma manages not to say anything to that, but her
silence about my father is as starchy as her apron.

I did not know so until the letters, but the vendetta between my father and my grandmother was already raging. The message inevitably has gone out to Wally from Grandma: *Charlie doesn't have much to say to me but I'm used to that now.* All the later years of my growing up, trying to solve the world of consequences brought on by this pernicious feud, I hunted wildly in the two of them for the reason. Did our Arizona trip itself set things off, Bessie Ringer with two sons gone to the war simply finding it the last straw that my mother was moving so far away? My grandmother had endured beyond other last straws. No, my in-the-dark guess was that the mysterious matter of family itself, its specific weight and gravity, brought on their wrangle. In the Faulkner Creek ranch years, there had chronically been a cluster of Ringers around, one or two and often all three of my mother's brothers working seasonal jobs for my father, and Grandma visiting every instant she could pry loose from the Norskie's chores. I figured my father then and there wore out on in-laws. But to my grandmother, after Moss Agate—because of Moss Agate?—family was the true tribe, she and the four kids bound together forever by having survived the utmost that my grandfather and the cow ghetto could bring down on them. If a Doig clan buckaroo married into the family, then he had simply been lucky enough to gain himself some family, by her notion of it.

So, the motives I found in those factions that I grew up between still howl true. As far as they go. What I was too near to my father and my grandmother to see was their greater ground of dispute, beyond a winter of veer to Arizona, beyond the ornery jousts of being in-laws. Their deadly tussle was over my mother.

". . . Not another cookie. Honest to Eleanor, Mom, you'll have him so spoiled . . ."

". . . Growing boy needs a little something to grow on, don't you, Ivan, yes . . ."

All said and done, although for an iron eon yet it would not be, the contest of spite between my grandmother and my father was about treatment of my mother. Nothing to do with medical terms, nor in any physical or even emotional sense; one thing neither could ever accuse the other of was lack of pure devotion to the girl and woman Berneta. Call it the geography of risk, of how best to situate my mother. My grandmother desperately wished that my parents (my father) would simply choose some-place in Montana—right about across the road from her would be ideal—and hunker in there at whatever the job happened to be and hope for the best. Surely-for-gosh-sakes it couldn't be good for Berneta to be living here, there, and everywhere, could it? To my father, just as desperately trying out footings until one felt secure for us, the worse risk was to sink so economically low we couldn't afford my mother's medical costs and whatever else might help her. He saw permanent ranch wagework as more of the mire of Moss Agate for her, and surely-to-Jesus-H.-Christ that can't be the best anybody can do, can it?

". . . sure awful glad, dear, to have you back where . . ."

". . . couldn't tell beforehand how Phoenix . . ."

Now comes the moment my mother has been bracing

toward ever since we arrived on this visit. My grandmother wants to know where next; where my mother and
my father and I will spend the summer.

"Gee gosh, Berneta!" Grandma lets out when told,
which from her is high-octane blue language. "I dread
to think of you out there!"

"We don't know for absolute sure we're going," is
resorted to by my mother the daughter. "Maybe something closer will turn up."

"You just get back from old Arizona and then you're
gone to out there." It is the mark of my grandmother
that she can blurt this and yet not have it scald out as
complaint or blame or pain or plea, but simply her
thought of the moment. The headturn of her endurance
toward what needed to be faced next.

I help myself to the cookie plate, in child's sly wisdom
that another oatmeal cookie or two won't even weigh in
the scale of what's occurring around me just now. My
mother is busy telling my grandmother whatever good
sides she can of our next notional move. My grandmother
would dearly like to be reassured but, with a catch in her
throat, at last can't help but sound her worst warning:

"You be careful with yourself, dear."

To that my mother utters nothing, for answer is none.
If careful could make a great enough difference in the
chokehold in her lungs, then that most enormous leap of
care, my father's uprooting of us to the lenient altitude
and climate of Arizona, ought to have done it. What
Berneta Ringer, now Berneta Doig, has grasped out of
the discard of her Moss Agate girlhood is the conviction
that she all too easily could careful herself into being an
invalid; that the triple pillows of asthma could coax away

her days as well as her nights if she didn't adamantly stay upright on the ground, heart-chosen ground. If this constituted reckless, this seemed what she still wanted to be.

"Careful as I can be, Mom," she sizes it down for my grandmother. "Anyway, we'll write," she announces as if letters will be the reward packets for our vanishing over one more horizon. Suddenly my mother gathers me away from the cookie plate in a big tickling hug, laughing, holding hard to me.

"Ivan and I will write you, won't we, kiddo."

MAUDLOW
MAY
14
PM
1945
MONT.

Dear Wally—
It is surely nice to know that the
Germans are taken care of, anyway.

December 25, 1962. Orange as an ember, the canyon plow slips out onto deserted Highway 12 and skims west through an hour ago's snow. Here at the rumbling start of its plowing run the huge bladed truck appears to be grooving a pathway into the crystal heart of a cloud, the highway only barely creasing the snowed-over sagebrush flatland. But this first stretch west of the highway maintenance section house is merely the top-of-the-stairs landing before the road dives between Grass Mountain and Mount Baldy, dropping and dropping like twisty cellar steps, nearly twenty unremitting miles of curves and constrictions. Winterlong, Wally drives the plow down the canyon of Deep Creek as many times of day and night as needed.

Beside Wally in the truck cab perches my father, guest passenger for this dusk run before Christmas supper. (I am in bellicose Texas, activated to an air force base there during the Cuban missile crisis.) A blue cigarette haze of truce accompanies the men; they both smoked like a fire in a coffin factory. Otherwise as unalike as brothers-in-law chronically are, the two of them get along when they're out like this; a loose fit, somewhere outdoors, has always been the best between the Doigs and the Ringers. There in the snowshoving truck my uncle and my father are still pleased with themselves and each other from their hunting season that autumn, the pinnacle day when, with Wally's ten- and twelve-year-old sons Dan and Dave along, they got into a herd of elk on an open slope in the Castle Mountains and blazed away, taking three big bulls in a minute's marksmanship. Dad's aging little Jeep was their hunting vehicle. Somehow the two men and two boys crammed the most massive elk, nearly horse-size, behind the seats, antlers out the tailgate like bizarre table legs; then strapped the other two beasts across the hood, drew a deep breath and started down the mountain with their ton and a half of elk. Instantly the Jeep's brakes gave up. Dad managed to swerve sideways to a stop, peered down the miles of mountainside to the Smith River Valley below and told Wally his nerves were not quite up to this. Taking over (I can see him grin a little at the windshieldful of elk carcass, hear him give out another of those pronouncements you could always count on: "The main thing is, not to get excited"), Wally hunched his brawn over the steering wheel and crept the Jeep into motion, groaning the load of wild meat down the mountain in low gear.

My father was sixty-one years old that autumn, and with the bad turns of health ahead of him, the elk bonanza was his last great hunt. Now, in the canyon plow, he is keen for another wizardly drive by Wally. Familied up for Christmas, the two men share a past bigger than their in-house divisions from each other. Snow-tented Grass Mountain ahead is something mutual too, Wally's recreational horizon every working day here on his section of highway, my father's remembered summer mountain from the herding honeymoon with my mother. But on this run of the snowblade, what my father looks forward to most of all is the defeat of Deep Creek Canyon, the one piece of earth I ever knew him to despise. To look at, Deep Creek is a beauty. Summoned by the Missouri River in the Broadwater Valley ahead, the clear creek speeds along within touch of the road, tumbling rhythmically down white steps of elevation, bumping raucously past rockfaced cliffs and between mountain vees of forest, pretty as can be pictured; but as a driver you are inside a snake. "I'd rather take a beating than drive that damn canyon," my father forever declared of this gauntlet he went through during the years of hospital dashes to Townsend with my mother. Deep Creek engorged us as quick as we returned from Arizona in 1945. *Took us 4 hours to come home* after a supper visit to our relatives in Townsend, my mother wrote to the young Pacific version of Wally. *The gas line on the car was plugged and we'd go about a mile, then get out and blow the thing out with the tire pump*, all this to be imagined in blackest night with other cars hurtling around Deep Creek's blind curves at our gasping Ford.

My father has never been rapid to credit any Ringer except my mother, but he swears that Wally could drive this treacherous canyon blindfolded. He gets a particular charge out of Wally's latest stunt with the canyon plow. The highway safety engineers have busily installed reflector posts to mark the shoulders of the road all through the canyon; these are in the way whenever Wally goes to shove a snowdrift off the road, so he has demonstrated to Dad how he is eliminating Deep Creek's new metal posts one by one, accidentally-on-purpose dropping the wingplow at just the right instant to clip a post off at its base and send it zinging up into the timber like a phosphorescent arrow.

At the head of the canyon, my father sits forward to watch, and my uncle gears down the tons of truck and blade. The snowplow starts down the brink beside Grass Mountain into the first curves of Deep Creek and commences zigzagging.

When the German half of World War Two was taken care of in May 1945, V-E Day couldn't even find my father and my mother and me by radio.

As you can see from our address, a map speck called Maudlow which actually was seven miles from us, *we have moved again*, on into my father's second season of sheepwork that spring, *lambing for Frank Morgan*. Our chosen land this time was that eye-taking rough horizon where the Big Belt Mountains and the Bridger Mountains butt up against each other.

The Morgan ranch buildings nestled on the Bridger side of this colliding geography, which is to say the prosperous side. Out the back door of the ranch stood the northmost Bridger peaks, Blacktail and Horsethief and Hatfield, but at its threshhold the land took a running start down to the Gallatin valley, fertile as a green dream. Based there on the rim of the broad Gallatin, the Morgans could afford to use the high country only for summer pasture and the rest of the year simply be thankful they were down out of the mountains' commotions of weather. To my parents, whose Big Belt history had been high country or higher, bad weather or worse, this was velvet ranching.

Charlie wrangles bunches, spends some time with the drop band, works in the lambing shed, in fact anything there is to do. Naturally my father is going like a house afire, but he isn't the only one who feels the green vim of the Gallatin country. *Ivan goes wrangling sheep with Charlie after supper. . . . He is growing, getting tall.* My mother herself is in charge of the Morgan cookhouse this staccato month of May. *I have 7 to cook for.* Twenty-one appetites a day don't faze her—*seem to have plenty of time so far*— but our mute radio does. *Sent for a battery. A person hates to be without a radio when there are so many things happening.* Elderly Frank Morgan and his son Horace are wonders to work for, ranch bosses who pitch in at all tasks themselves in a style that shames the baronial Smith River country. *Mr. Mor. hardly stops a minute, sure gets a lot done for a man his age.* Because the war is still on, the Morgan lambing crew is short-handed and my mother views a couple of them as short in the head, too. *The kid herding the drop band,* the maternity ward of ewes, *has a saddle horse and he never gets off all day long outside of to eat lunch.* I fabulously come into wealth when Frank Morgan promises ten dollars to anybody who kills a coyote, Dad's rifleshot bowls one over, but the corpse can't be found. *Charlie said he didn't want the money as he couldn't produce the coyote, so Mr. Mor. gave the money to Ivan.* Winona pops in for a weekend visit and sets off flutters among the bachelor ranch hands. *Did she tell you one of the sheepherders fell for her?* my mother can't resist passing along to Wally. *Poor Winona, we razzed her so much.* When did any of us ever sleep?

*　　*　　*

Maudlow, though. Any tinier and it would have been microscopic, any more remote and it would have been off the planet. Maudlow was the deepest depot along the Milwaukee Railroad's route through the stubborn canyons of the Big Belts, a maintenance spot which had accrued a post office and a store of sorts. Here around the corner from the Bridger Mountains, the country went wild in a hurry. Hardly anybody possessed the mental compass to settle in this isolated bottom end of the Big Belts. Even my mother from none too cosmopolitan Moss Agate and Ringling called the Maudlow country *the sticks*.

Maudlow mattered because of the summer ahead of us.

I never saw such muddy roads in my life and as you know we've traveled some pretty muddy ones.

The storm is coming toward us on lightning stilts. *CRACKuunnggg*, the thunder-and-echo.

"Rain some more, why don't ye," my father responds from the mudhole where the Ford sits axle-deep.

We want to get a horse pasture fixed up and a few odd jobs done, but all we did was get out of town as far as the Dave Winter place and got stuck.

My mother waits behind the steering wheel, wearing the look that says she and muddy roads do not get along. I am out of the car clumping around in her overshoes, not about to miss this chance to wallow in the mire in an almost official capacity.

And actually, if you have to be stuck hubcap deep in mud, this is a scenic spot for it. Willows cluster nearby in testimony of the seep of springwater that causes the mudhole. Wild roses and wild carrot and lupine bloom around. Nor, in spite of an absence of other people for fifteen miles in either direction, are we alone. Gophers are plentiful that rainy spring, and a hawk is having a feast. Silently drifting down he makes his grab and flies off, the snatched gopher's back legs pedaling in air.

"Try it now, Berneta," my father directs, standing on the Ford's back bumper hoping his 130 pounds will add vast traction. "Just give it the littlest bit of gas—"

"I know."

"—until it starts going—"

"Charlie, I *know*."

"—and then gun it."

While my father bounces energetically on the bumper, my mother eases down on the gas pedal as if trying to tiptoe out of trouble, but the back wheels spin like greased tornadoes.

"No good," my father calls a halt to my mother's accelerator foot and hops down off the bumper, fresh freckles of mud all over him. He chews the inside of his mouth as he tries to see through buttes to Maudlow, a lot of miles away, and then in the other direction to Ringling, just as many miles. Closer than either is the coming island of lightning, thunder, and rain. My mother appears distinctly unsurprised at the verdict my father reaches.

Had to jack the car up, put boards under it.

The boards are the old Dave Winter homestead, collapsing at the foot of a butte about a quarter of a mile from us. My mother makes me sploosh back to the car so she can have her overshoes, administers me into my own, which seem even more babyish now after the roominess of hers, and the two of us march out of the mudhole. My father is waiting for us, barely, at the brow of the little dip that holds the mudhole. Here we all take off our overshoes, because they're not needed on the shaley ground across to the old Winter place; the Maudlow road has the monopoly on mud.

At the Winter buildings we scavenge fast, plucking boards from the dilapidated sheepshed and anywhere else we can find loose ones. What's left of the windowless house of this homestead, though, we studiously avoid in our plunder; Dave Winter in his time had married into the Doigs, and so this house of his is in a way us, too.

Back to the mudhole we totter with our armloads of boards. Our overshoes are there waiting for us like three sizes of floppy puppies.

Hurrying to beat the rain, we ferry the boards to the car and my father seizes the widest one and lays it into the soupy area beneath the rear bumper as a base to set the jack on. He rolls his sleeves to the elbow. "Time for the Armstrong method," he says as general encouragement. However frazzled the rest of my father may be, his arms always are strong and they now pump the jack handle vigorously, *whup*-down *whup*-down *whup*-down. During these exertions my mother stands arms-crossed and watches him as if trying to reach a diagnosis.

Charlie feels pretty good most of the time. Says he gets a pain in his side once in awhile, but not often.

When Dad stands up from the bumper jack to rest for a moment, my mother steps in and teeters her full weight, such as it is, on the jack handle. The jack head ratchets slowly up and catches in the next higher notch, ratchets up another oh so slow notch when she does it again. She manages to contribute half a dozen notches up the jack stem before my father judiciously takes over again.

No matter who works the jack handle, though, the rear bumper rises very little but the board submerges steadily. My father cusses, releases the jack, and layers more boards on top of the first one.

This time the jacking brings up the entire back of the car enough to slip boards lengthwise under the tires, and, the first spits of rain beginning to find us, the three of us hastily lay paths of boards in the ruts ahead far enough— we hope—to give us a running start out of the mudhole.

This time my father mans the gas pedal and steering wheel. The Ford shoots ahead the length of the first-laid boards, onto the next set, then slews off and drops, mired, again. My father cusses and we all climb out to start over on the jacking.

CRACK!

—from a lightning bolt striking the butte nearest us.

"Ivan, get in the car, right now," my mother commands, flinging the passenger-side door open and poising to follow me in. "Charlie . . . ?"

Even in a fuming mood, my father knows enough to listen to thunder that is too close to cast an echo. He ducks into the coupe on the driver's side as more lightning slams to earth not very far away, and here we are in the insulating rubber-tired Ford. Grounded, in numerous meanings of the word.

Again we perform the kicking off of overshoes, as the rain tapping on the car roof lets us know it is going to be around for a while. I promptly squirm into the back-seat and ledge myself crosswise in the rear window, a la Arizona. I find I don't fit as well as I did. True, there'd been enough rain in the Maudlow country this spring to shrink the Ford, but I knew I was growing, outgrowing. Lying curled against the car glass, this is maybe my final chance to childspy on the mysteries in the front seat.

My father lights a cigarette to try to bribe his nerves. Then he contemplates the ruts ahead, troughs of brown jelly. "We could use about a hundred feet of that Arizona desert just now."

My mother says nothing.

My father's Stetson is damp and he takes it off and crimps the crown and brim here and there to make sure it keeps the crease he likes. Under the disguise of that comes his question.

"Ye feeling all right, are you?"

I've been having a little more asthma, her report to Wally during the strenuous Morgan lambing season just past, *but not so bad*.

"Tuckered out on mud, is all," my mother answers. "When we get through being stuck, let's don't fight this road any more today."

My father weighs that. Beyond the mudhole are the day's chores that all need doing: fixing the fence of the saddle pasture, then rounding up into it the necessary horses of summer, Tony, Duffy, Sugar, Star.

"Berneta, we need to lay hold of those damn horses."

"This isn't getting it done."

My father inspects the rain pittering onto the wind-shield and now he says nothing.

Bunked where I am, I carefully stay more silent than their silence.

Sure as the world, my father rouses to the weather, the freshening season. "All this rain is bringing the grass, ye have to say that for it."

He smokes as if thinking over something my mother had just asked. "We can come out good on this sheep deal, don't ye think?"

The sheep deal. It has been in the air all the way back to Wickenburg. My father had not given up on Arizona for good, in those desert nights of talking things over, but he'd discerned that he had to be stronger in his wallet and a few other parts of himself to niche us a new life there. The other side of the Arizona mirror went toward north: one more mountain summer in Montana, a last high season of livestock while they were drawing fancy prices. The sheep of war. In a band of sheep—a thousand ewes, their thousand and some lambs, and their wool— you were looking at a profit of several thousand dollars, and these were dollars of 1945. Wages would never add up that fast, even if they could be found and hung onto. *Would be nice here for the summer*, my mother allowed herself to pine momentarily at the Morgan cookhouse near the end of that spring, *trees in the yard*, *a lilac bush out in front*. But the capable Morgans ran their ranch by themselves once lambing was over, and she recognized that by the first of June we would have to put our belongings in the Ford again. Somehow, summer had to be mined for all it was worth. So when my father began to think out loud about a sheep deal, she was ready to listen. *Looks like we should be able to make quite a little money at it*. The sheep deal was a masterpiece of carvery. Dad and his favorite brother, Angus, a good business head, went in together and bought the band of a thousand ewes and their new lambs from Frank Morgan, turned right around and sold them for delivery that fall. Shearing time came before that, so the wool money came to us and Angus. But the summer range to run the sheep on needed to be rented from the Morgans, at so much per head; on the other hand, Dad would ameliorate that charge with some work for the Morgans—

When everybody had taken every whittle they could out of the hypothetical profits, up we would go into the high country with the actual band of sheep.

"Looks like," letter becoming life in the dreamchamber of the Ford, "we should be able to make quite a little money at it," my mother repeats her vote for the sheep deal, for the summer of calculated risk we are trying to get to. "Give you a chance to take life a little easy, too."

"What, easier than this?" my father indicates our immobile condition. "Just sitting here letting the tires rest?"

"I'll rest you," my mother rejoins. I can't see her smile, but her voice has it.

"This sheep deal, Berneta." This comes serious, pledgelike, from my father. "If it ever gets to be too much for ye, we'll back down out of there."

"Don't worry, I hired out to be tough," she heads him off on that. She makes a fist and rubs a hole in the breath fog on her window to peek at the weather.

"See there, the rain's letting up," my father points out. "Ivan, you're not having much to say for yourself. What do ye think, ready to build some more road?"

Back to the jacking, and trying to roof the ruts with

boards, a task which I adore. Then a miracle. *Bob Campbell*, one of Dad's army of Scotch relatives riding the Big Belt coulees, *happened along on a saddle horse and gave us a pull, and we finally did get out.*

As he coils his lariat Bob Campbell tells us what we already have figured out, that any passing shadow of a cloud is enough to turn the Maudlow country into a gumbo quagmire. Then he cheerily wishes us luck and resumes his riding. Which again leaves the three of us, and the nearby homestead-haunted butte, and the horizon mountains, a bit farther from us than usual, of our past. Such home as we have is this country where my parents are trying and trying to taste the risk for each other. Married to the place.

MAUDLOW
JUNE
15
PM
1945
MONT.

Dear Wally—
The herder we had planned on lost 30
lambs in about 10 days, so at that rate
we'd have to buy him another band of
lambs by fall.

For the first time in half a year, Berneta's letters seem to catch their breath.

June 8, 15, and 19, 1945. Her glad reports begin with what neighbored our meadow cabin on the face of Hatfield Mountain, *a nice stream*. Where my father, *getting caught up on his fishing*, made its waters our supperland of rainbow trout. Almost as softly as if talking to herself, she puts to the pages the three of us starting up our spiral staircase of summer.

We aren't working very hard at present. Were out for a horseback ride this afternoon, first time I've been on a horse for ages. Ivan & I rode Duffy, Charlie rode Sugar. That tandem ride likely was our last; this was the getting-big-for-my-britches period when I took it into my head to require not only a horse all my own but the ruggedest possible saddle, a sawbuck packframe, for myself.

Received our band of sheep last Mon. Nice bunch of lambs, 1230 of them. Sure hope they weigh good this fall and we can keep the loss down. . . .

We have a herder for now, but when the sheep go on the Forest Reserve the 1st of July or about, Charlie, Ivan & I may herd them. We aren't sure yet. Charlie is going up to look at the Reserve range & see how tough it is. . . .

*Don't know just yet when we will shear. I shouldn't have
a lot of work to do after shearing, and that should only last
one day unless a rainstorm catches us. . . .*

*Ivan is busy drawing pictures. Does pretty good. He'll
soon have a birthday, doesn't seem possible he'll be six. . . .*

When my father shouldered open the door of that
cabin of then, packhorses and wife and child and twenty-
two hundred sheep at his back, a mouse nest fell down
onto the brim of his Stetson. Ceiling paper drooped in
shreds. The greenblinds on the windows were speckled
with mashed flies, the floor was soiled with mouse drop-
pings and pack rat leavings.

The place was a sty, but not for long. The floor of a
housing project cubicle on the factory outskirts of Phoenix, maybe Berneta would wash with tears. But this cabin
on the summer mountain she launched into with soapy
water. Led by the hurricane broom of my father, who
cocked a look out every window he swept past to check
on the behavior of the sheep.

To dream us this last time, into the twists of June, I
harbor there at the very first hours of the swabbed cabin.

And watch Berneta as she gives her mop a conclusive
wring. On the go, beds and plenty else to be seen to, she
brushes by the foot of the scant cot beneath the southmost
window and sings out, "Ivan, look how you'll just fit."
I inspect, solemnly bob my head, and claim the bunk
with my tarp-wrapped bedroll. A corner of my own, all
I ask. My parents will share the plank-sided bed in the
opposite corner, snug for two but they do not seem to
mind the prospect. No pillows to this sheepcamp exis-

tence, so Berneta mounds our three mackinaw jackets at the head of her side of the bed to prop herself against asthma in the night.

Bleary windowpanes to be washed next. Berneta debates to herself whether to do away with the nasty greenblinds—nobody for five miles around to see in on us—but ends up scouring the fly matter off them. Blank windows have never seemed right to her.

Even though the morning outside is wearing its summer best—*hasn't rained the last 2 or 3 days, really seems good to see some sunshine*—I tag after Berneta there in the cabin. Follow her eyes while she inventories this domestic side of the sheep deal, the three-month one-room future. The cookstove is frankly puny, a midget two-lid job not much more than kneehigh even on her, but it will fire up fast and then not hold hot through these summer days. The elderly table, scarred and stained from extra duty as a butcher block, at least presides at the proper window, the west one which lets in a good view of the willow course of the creek. Across the room, the canned-goods cupboard for once is huge enough, homemade logic of someone who, like her, has needed to store away most of a season of groceries at a time. And she is glad of the smaller cool cupboard, the outside cabinet of shelves handy beside the door and tinned against rodents; leftovers will keep for a day or so in there, and for longer term, butter and cheese and any grouse my father manages to hunt can be sealed in jars and coldstored in the creek.

Could be worse, her kitchen veteran's appraisal and our recent history of the drab White Sulphur Springs house and drabber Alzona Park both say. At the other end of the cabin's single room hunkers a heating stove big as a blast furnace, so close to the main bed that it seems to be trying to sneak under the covers. Winter here halfway up a Montana alp must be icily beyond even what we were accustomed to at the Faulkner Creek ranch, according to the double set of stoves only a dozen feet apart and the triplicate cabin walls—broad rough boards undermost, then clapboard siding nailed to their outside, and a surprisingly cozy interior of short boards pieced together bricklike—and the roof of corrugated tin sheeting for snow to slide off. We are summering here, not wintering. Could be worse.

My father tromps in with a heaping armload of firewood, goes to dump it in the woodbox, lets the wood thunder down next to the box instead of into it. "We're going to have to get after the pack rats, first thing," he declares as he scoops out of the woodbox yet another junk trove accumulated by them. Marauders so quizzical, swiping a torn handkerchief one night, a thimble the next, you had to wonder if they did it from sense of humor.

The trapper Berneta kids him, "So if I catch them, think that'll make them easy enough for you to shoot?" Two scabbards are slung on my father's saddlehorse. In one, the .22 rifle that is the shooting machine for pack rats and grouse. In the other, his .30–06 coyote artillery.

"Other way around, any I shoot first ye can sneak up and clamp a trap on, can't ye," he gives her back and starts lugging in the contents tarp-wrapped on our pack saddles.

Groceries to the big cupboard, enough to last until the Morgan camptender begins weekly provisioning. Our change of shirts and pants onto tenpenny nails spiked in a row on the wall next to the door. Washbasin, floursack towel. Frying pan and tin plates and pair of cooking pots and a dishpan. Utensils and box of wooden matches and lantern. Luxury item, a flashlight. Habitation is 95 percent habituation, so the cabin begins to seem familiar as soon as our own clutter is in place. Rexall drugstore calendar to keep track of the days. Small pane of mirror on the washstand for my father to shave by, Berneta to groom by. Our own galvanized bucket for our drinking water, because there's no telling what has visited any bucket you find in a disused cabin.

My father, everywhere today, is at the barn unsaddling the horses. I hesitate. But Berneta too has reached a last chore, stretching to arrange her writing materials on the top shelf of the tin-lined cool cupboard, the only place where stationery and black little bottle of ink and her inscribed fountain pen can be safe until the pack rats are dealt with. I unmoor from the completed cabin and speed out toward the saddle side of things.

Outdoors here is more elaborate than in. The cabin site is cuddled against the girth of the Bridger Mountains like a tyke on a giant lap. All directions from this perched place, you see to forest-tipped peaks of Bridgers or Big Belts and grassed ridgebacks of fetching green; view, view, view, gangs of views. Nearly three twisty miles by horseback down the gulch is the Maudlow road, where the Ford sits stashed behind chokecherry bushes. The timberline of the Gallatin National Forest, with its Reserve range where the sheep can graze come July, stands in back of the cabin another couple of miles, mainly up. High country and higher, this nestled but abandoned homestead, even by Doig and Ringer standards. The place has the feel of getting away with something, pulling a trick at odds with the surrounding geography. The ever so level deck of meadow; how in the world did that slip in here between convulsive gulches that nearly stand on end? Then the cabin knoll, just enough of an ascension to lord it over the meadow; terrace in the wilderness, no less? And the water helling off down the gulch is a surprising amount of creek, yet its flow is disguised away, hidden beneath steep banks until you peek straight down into the disturbed glass of its riffles.

Barn smells never masquerade, though. Musty hay and leathery harness and almost neutral old manure tinge the air as I clock in on my father and the saddle stock. Unexpected as a chateau, the steep-peaked barn holds stalls for all four horses and there even were enough fenceposts around it, askew but still standing, to resurrect a pasture. Liberated from the chore of picketing Sugar and Duffy and Tony and Star on thirty-foot ropes, Dad moves through the unsaddlings whistling the same chorus over and over in pleasure.

He and I emerge to the cabin knoll again, and the next unexpected construction.

"Daddy, the outy is logs!"

"That's a new one on me," he has to admit. So heftily overbuilt is the log outhouse that it's more like a blockhouse, ponderous and immovable. "He must've wanted to make sure it wouldn't pick up and run away," my father says as if he knew such cases. An earlier Charlie had striven on this mountain shelf of earth. Bachelor homesteader Charles Rung, who applied himself enough to assemble the cabin and the barn and the preposterously redoubtable toilet, but his intended two-story house was still stacked as lumber, a mighty pile of weathered boards sitting neatly amid the weeds. The Morgans, maybe half-way meaning it, had joked to us that they bought old Rung out for that stack of lumber, with the rest of the place thrown in. Not much known about Rung, said the Morgans. He filed his homestead claim back in the time of World War One, slaved away at the place except to get a little money ahead as a field hand in the Gallatin Valley grain harvest some years; wintered all by his lone-some in here. Whoever he'd been, Charlie Rung had some knack for putting up with his own company in style. In the timber of the gulch a little way from the cabin was his cache-hole where he stashed homebrewed wine and the venison he shot out of season, which was to say virtually all the time.

On our way across the knoll from the barn to the cabin, my father can't help but stop for a minute and palm his hands into his hip pockets, happily proprietary as he scans the gray grazing band. The sheep can't believe their good luck. They stand in their tracks gobbling the lush meadow grass like a serving of hay, then plunge ahead three quick steps to gorge the same way, time and again. By noon they are so roly-poly they don't even head for the brush to shade up, simply flump down in the open meadow.

Our own meal, this first cabin lunchtime, is Spam sandwiches, drawing the accusation from my father that it's a plot to send him directly out fishing. Berneta teases back that that sounds to her like the right idea.

But both stay sat, in the beginning of the afternoon, and quietly take in the cabin, the country outside, this first stairstep of summer. Our reward to ourselves after the Spam is Kool-Aid, the family passion for lime-flavor glinting green in our three tin cups. As if he's just thought of something, my father leans across the table toward the window to check the position of the sun, then compares the alignment of the cabin. "At least the place sits straight with the world," he verifies. What is it that arranged us this way in our thinking: the squares of a mile each that the land in the West was surveyed into, the section-line roads that rulered us wherever we drove in that country, the boxlike rural rooms fitting no other logic? Whatever ingrained edge it is, to this day I have some of the family unease with any house whose axis angles off from a compass reading of absolute north-south or east-west.

The cabin wasn't through with my father. He tips his chair back and aims his most studying look at where the door stands open, pleasant cool of noon breezing in. "But what the hell was he thinking of with a north door?" North is storm country, snow and blow waiting to swarm in any time you reach for the doorknob between November and April.

Berneta sends her gaze out the rickety screen door, down the lunge of gulch toward the Maudlow road. "Bet you a milkshake I can guess why," she mischievously arrives at. "He wanted a good long look at who was coming."

My father chuckles at her point about that other Charlie, the in-season-and-out homesteader Rung. "Like maybe a game warden, could be."

So, straight with the world or not, we've come to rest in notorious territory. Not simply in terms of the comatose old homestead's history of contraband venison, ei-

ther. Where we are, this start of June, is the extremity
of the Sixteen country. Under those horizon-bumping
views from this meadow, Sixteenmile Creek scampers
through the confused geography from every direction,
the main channel twisting down from the Wall Mountain
basins in the north and skewing west to its union with
the Missouri River, joined midway by the Middle Fork
shooting in from the east and the Ringling country
through a sharp canyon. Then there is a last, orphan
section of the creek springing from entirely different
drainage, the sly tether of the Big Belts to the Bridger
range. The stream streaking down our gulch is that off-
shoot, the South Fork of Sixteenmile Creek. Behind us,
Hatfield Mountain of the Bridgers sits like a mile-tall
apartment building facing down on the rock alleys of
the Big Belts. We are in for a climbing summer, the
saddlehorses huffing constantly on the slopes behind the
cabin, we know that much. But the meadows of the back
of the lofty Bridgers are going to be worth it—such
grass, this rain-fed early summer, that the sheep will
fatten on it as if it were candied.

Dogs, we're rife with dogs again.

Sheepdogs, at least in theory; Flop with a wonderful
half-mast ear that begs affection and Jack with the pale
eyes, barely blue, of a born chaser.

Even my father can find no grounds to object to their
instant conversion by Berneta into housedogs, because it
just as fast becomes plain that only one or the other can
be used on the sheep each day. When the two dogs are
worked together, they add up to less than one. Jack sulks

whenever Flop is sent around the sheep with him, Flop takes a yipping fit any time he is held back from a mission with Jack.

"Whoever invented dogs," my father appraised this nerved-up pair, "has a hell of a lot to answer for."

But perhaps our prima donna canines figured they were putting in their shifts just as much as anybody else. *Charlie has been watching the sheep early in the morns. & late in the eves. while the herder gets his meals*, ran Berneta's latest report to the *Ault*. The sheep deal had advanced to a phase known as tepee herding. Day-and-night sentry duty with the band of sheep because of coyotes and the tough terrain, it amounted to. Occupied enough with settling us in at the Rung place and trying to gauge Berneta's hardiness and readying for shearing and thinking over a big haying contract that was being dangled (*Walter Donahoe wants us to put up the hay on the Loophole*—back in the White Sulphur Springs country—*again, but don't know whether we will be able to take that on*), even my father couldn't find a second twenty-four hours in the day to spend with the sheep and was resorting to a hired herder. The one who came recommended didn't seem to be any whiz—"I wouldn't call him the greatest," Dad left it at—but he trooped through the day with the sheep as required and bedded down on the mountain with them every night without complaints. Except for those turns at sheepwatching while the herder fed himself, we had only to move the herder's tepee to a new bedground for each night and generally supervise.

"Pretty easy living," Dad has to admit as he and I bounce back into the cabin, day of our own yet ahead, after a morning shift with the sheep.

"About time you tried some," Berneta ratifies with a pleased look up from the letter she is writing.

This lasted an entire week and a half, until the morning my father and I found a lamb gut-eaten by a coyote practically at the doorflap of the herder's tepee.

The instant the sheep shaded up at midday my father was sifting his way into them on a walkthrough count of the lambs. Tricky to do, step by ever so slow step, negotiating a route without roiling the sheep. Low at his hip, his right hand flicks its little stroke of arithmetic at each lamb he tallies, and every time a hundred is reached his left thumbnail gouges a mark in the soft wood of his pocket pencil.

His walkthrough marks out at twelve hundred lambs, thirty short of what we had handed over to the tepee herder just ten days ago. (*At that rate we'd have to buy him another band of lambs* . . .) This herder is a scenery inspector, idling away under tree or tepee while the coyotes have been using the band as a meat market.

My father wheeled, strode over to the herder and snapped, "Roll your damned bed."

The next herder, escorted in by the Morgan camptender, my parents immediately dub Prince Al for his rapidfire consumption of Prince Albert tobacco. When he isn't smoking the twisty shreds from the red can, he chews the stuff. Brown parentheses of snoosejuice, apparently permanent, hang at the corners of his mouth, but what really catches attention are the tracks of his roll-your-own habit down the front of his shirt, the burn specks where dribbles of ash fall from his handmade cigarettes. My father is heard to mutter we'll be lucky if this one doesn't burn down the mountain and the sheep with it.

Dad and I are barely back from moving the herder's tepee the first morning when rifleshots break out on the mountain behind us. *KuhWOW! KuhWOW-kuhWOW-kuhWOW.*

Naturally I was all in favor of any form of bombardment, but my father the coyote marksman listens skeptically to the herder's fusillade. If you don't knock over a coyote with your first shot you're probably wasting your lead.

Berneta appears out of the cabin to cock an ear at the uproar. "Makes you wonder if the coyotes are shooting back at him, doesn't it."

When the three of us ride up that evening, we see that the sheep and Jack the dog are as jittery as if they, not the coyotes, have been under barrage all day. Not that any casualties can be counted among the coyotes. Prince Al, it develops, has the philosophy of touching off a shot whenever a stump or a shadow looks as if it conceivably *might* be a coyote. My father tells him that's an interesting theory, but how about saving his ammunition unless he's goddamn-good-and-sure about the target.

The next morning, Dad and I just reach the cabin when a new salvo of *kuhWOW*s thunders from the mountainside.

Very soon the Jack dog comes arcing across the meadow in a neurotic slink, belly to the ground as if begging us *please don't blame me please I simply can't take any more of that commotion* until ending up, inevitably, under Berneta's merciful petting hand.

She and I watch my father with apprehension.

He, though, seems downright gratified to see the deserter dog. "We'll just let Mister Prince Al have a day of handling those sheep without a dog. See if that slows him up on the shooting."

By that evening, having chased after sheep over half the Bridger Mountains, the herder was the frazzled one and the cannonading was cured.

But a few more days into Prince Al's term of herding, on the fifteenth morning of June, my father comes into the cabin disgusted. Right there with him as usual, I'm excited, a bit traitorously, by this latest bulletin.

"Can ye believe it," he lays it out for Berneta, "that scissorbill of herder has to have a trip to town already. Compensation papers of some kind he needs to fix up."

She too is getting her fill of wartime sheep help. "Quite an imposition on these herders, isn't it, to ask them to actually herd."

My father steams out the choices. Deny Prince Al the trip and he'll most likely quit the job. Or much worse, sulk for several days of misbehavior with the sheep and *then* quit. Hang onto Prince Al until shearing if we can, is the least nasty conclusion. The only virtue evident in him is the one that counts, he isn't losing lambs left and right.

"I better take the sheep tomorrow," my father brings himself around to the necessary, "while you run him in to Bozeman, how about." She has done this endless times before, ferrying a hired man so that a toothache or a case of boils or, as now, a pesky piece of government paper could be taken care of; for any ranch wife, as usual as a can of coffee on a grocery list. A day away from the Rung place, medicine against monotony, it provides too.

My father is going on, "It'll give you your chance at the mail and some fresh goods, and while you're in there do something nice for yourself and shop for—"

He stops. Berneta is shaking her head.

I'll play sheepherder tomorrow.

"What, instead of making the trip to town? How'd ye get that in your head?"

I'd rather herd than to take him in. The roads in this country get my goat.

My father rethinks. A possibly slippery drive through the Maudlow mudholes, versus a horseback day with the sheep for her. "That's what you'd really rather, is it." Then the central concern: "You're sure ye feel up to that?"

"I can get by with the herding," she reassures him. "The horse and the dog will do the most of it. Don't worry none, I'm not about to walk myself to death chasing after fool sheep."

She cheerfully turns to the matter of me. "Which for you, Ivan? Playing sheepherder or into town?"

I blink. It had never occurred to me the town trip might not include me. By now I am practically the child gazetteer of towns, Phoenix to Maudlow. Later it dawns on me, too late, that going herding with her would have been an entire dreamday aboard my own horse. But instead I choose horsepower, the Ford, habit of journey and whatever obtains: "Town, I guess."

*   *   *

The next morning my father and I and Prince Al slewed our way first of all into Maudlow. Maudlow gumbo: a bum go, Maudlow. Whipping the Ford's steering wheel this way and that, my father comes up with the sarcastic theory that the only reason the railroad was routed through this country was because the mud is thick enough to float a train. Prince Al, chawing away, mutely doesn't get it.

Six miles of slip and slide, and we tromp into the tiny Maudlow post office to collect our backed-up mail. Wally is heard from, Winona, Anna and Joe, of course my grandmother (three of those envelopes), four or five other friends or relatives, the weekly paper from White Sulphur Springs and a batch of my comic books which I would have read before we were out of the post office if Dad had let me. Berneta has hungered for these letters: *haven't had the mail for 2 wks. Went down to get it Tues. but the road was washed out this side of Maudlow.* Her letters in turn cascade into the Maudlow mail slot, away to the *Ault* goes her dispatch of us written just yesterday. *We are all pretty well. Some days I don't feel too good but can't complain most of the time.*

More mire, between us and Bozeman. The windshield keeps threatening to go blind from mudspots, so whenever my father guns the car through ruts of standing water he flips the wipers on after the splash. Dirty water to wash dirtier. The slap of the wipers sounds frantic, as if the Ford is trying to bat away the accumulating muck.

We smear our way past ranches now, fundamental sets of buildings, then the Morgans' workstained sheepshed. The arched backs of the Bridger Mountains slowly file along beside us.

Eventually the road drops, and drops some more, into an eyelet of gap between farmed ridges, and the Gallatin Valley opens up prosperously for twenty miles ahead.

Downhill now, glide all the way to the long main street of Bozeman. My father points out a field where as a young man he worked in the grain harvest. (Land that later grew four lanes of freeway and a Holiday Inn.) Downtown in Bozeman, we let Prince Al out at the government office and tackle our own chores. First thing, fill the Ford with gas; rationing still rules. Then something I was distinctly not keen on; under orders from Berneta, what my father calls getting our ears lowered.

Normally our haircuts were homemade, and a barbershop's fuss and strangenesses spooked me. Green eyeshade worn by the hovering barber; why put lime color atop the eyes, why not skyblue? The barber chair with those corrugated arm-ends as if the chair was enough of a participant to tense its own knuckles. The mirrors on the walls both in front and back of the haircut victim, I actually could see the use of; ease of glance for the barber so that he wouldn't snip you lopsided. But the surplus of reflections echoing away, where do those bounces ever stop and why don't they?

Even my hair seemed to know it was in odd circumstances. The barber tucked the whispery cloth in around my collar and critically combed my flop of red shag across my head. Then asks, as though it might matter in how he proceeds: "Where you fellows from?"

Where indeed, given our road record since the Ford was loaded and aimed to Arizona last November. But my father flaps a wrinkle out of the newspaper he is reading and encompasses everything from the root years of the

Doig homestead to the Morgan summer range of the moment. "We're out here on Sixteen—"

Sixteen kinds of weather a day this year, I can imagine Berneta saying to herself as she unties the yellow slicker from behind the saddle and slips it on. Knots the saddlestrings firmly down on the mackinaw jacket she'd been wearing since she left the cabin and climbs back on Duffy to ride through the sun shower, freshet of rain about the size of a sprinkler can's but thoroughly damp. Makes you wonder why June days need to be so unpredictable. Hour to hour there's the sense that summer is being invented over again, one sky after another.

She rides with a bit of deliberate jangle, from the ring of cans—empty condensed milk ones, strung on a loop of baling wire, which you shake for a clatter to make sheep hustle along—hung handy on her saddlehorn.

Ahead of her the trail zigs and zags up the mountain like a carpenter's rule unfolding. A quarter of the way up the mountainside, no, already more like a third of the way up, a mob of wool is expanding in many too many directions at once, helter-skelter. Say for Prince Al that he started the sheep out onto the big slope decently enough this morning, but their behavior is disintegrating in a hurry, and she and the horse and dog have to get right at it to head them off. She'd decided first thing to leave Jack leashed at the cabin and use Flop for the day, eagerness over temperament, and the bent-eared dog flirts sideways at her in gratitude as they travel the trail.

Ten minutes' hard climb by the saddlehorse carries Berneta through the rain climate—off with the slicker, back into the mackinaw—and up to where she feels she can start dealing with the herd situation. The sheep are full of run this morning. Every second minute, the lead ewes have to be turned, bent back from their abrupt mania to quit the country, stream out across the mountain just to be traveling. You'd think the fools had appointments somewhere. Here and there a bunchbreaker erupts, a solo sheep dithering off toward the tall timber with forty lambs following like a tail on a kite. The worst vagabond, a haughty high-headed ewe determined to stomp off back to the bedground, Berneta slings the ring of cans at and has the satisfaction of clouting her in the rump and causing a panicked veer back to the protection of the herd. Don't dare do much of that, as it means the exertion of climbing off and on the horse to retrieve your noisemaker, but it shows the old biddies you mean business.

She uses the dog to take the run out of them, directing him with backhand sweeps of her arm as if clearing away a curtain of air. "Go around them, Flop. Around them, boy." The dog races ahead of the sheep in short arcs, stopping every fifty yards or so to give her an *enough?* look. Ewes still are stubbornly squirting off in tangents of their own on the other side of the band from the dog, so Berneta keeps sending him on his rainbow dashes until he's circled the entire band. Just as obstinately as they'd been scattering to the four winds, the sheep now keg up, huddle there in a half-acre knot of wool blinking at her and the dog.

She catches her breath and, ugly though a noneating band of sheep wrapped around itself is to any self-respecting herder, she waits. And waits some more, facing down the twenty-two hundred saturnine sheepheads. Let them grow tired of being bunched up, the lunatics weren't gaining any grass into themselves anyway cantering off across creation the way they'd been.

The sheep mill a little in an unruly circle, eyeing the dog problem. All at once the whole bunch catches the inspiration to mother up with their lambs. The epidemic now is ewes sniffing furiously to make sure the offspring is their own, lambs diving to their knees to suckle. After the session of this, the band of sheep begins to graze up the slope as polite as you please.

Even when sheep are on their best behavior you don't simply lollop across the countryside with a band of them, especially if the country is as mountainy as this. Eight thousand eight hundred hooves to control, in a more or less simultaneous pursuit of grass, while avoiding coyotes and bear and deadfall snags and poisonous weeds and any other assassins that shadow the travels of sheep. Berneta sheds the mackinaw—coat on, coat off, that kind of day—and takes stock. Today's grazing territory is from the gulch on up the flank of Hatfield Mountain toward the timberline, then down again. "Bring them into camp tonight, let's do," Charlie had formulated with her. "Halfway up along there is a great plenty for the day, then swing them back down. I ought to have that geezer of a herder back here by the time you head them down." Which will mean, for her, seeing to it that the band grazes as far up as the halfway point on the mountainslope before shading up, then easing them in a half-circle turn back down this afternoon, toward the upper end of the cabin meadow for the night. Getting sheep to do anything by halves goes against their nature, but she hired out to herd for all she's worth, didn't she.

"That includes you, Duffy," she converses to the horse. "Let's go, boy."

As the horse answers that and the dig she gives him with her heels by grunting his way up the slope, Berneta is glad her body is becoming accustomed to the saddle again. Getting toward toughened in, although not entirely there yet. Already, this early, she can notice that horsework is work for the rider too. She always marvels at Charlie. Beat up as he is in various parts of himself, he can climb on a horse and go at it all day without ever feeling an effect.

The sheep fan out a little as she wants them to, their interest perfectly where it ought to be, one clump of grass to the next. She reins up beside the hooved cloud, her horse pointed upslope a certain neck-bowed way, herself posed attentive to the moment a certain way, and it happens. The years peel away and she is the photographed horsewoman again, arch of a mountain framing her. Some differences; there always are. Here, she is dressed not for the camera lens but for the job; workshirt, workpants, work*shoes* that she knows she must be careful not to thrust through the stirrup when climbing on even imperturbable-seeming old Duffy—one of Charlie's worst poundings hit him when his horse shied at a snake as he was mounting and the stirrup snared his foot through to the ankle, dragging him like a gunnysack alongside the kicking hooves of the runaway. Nor is she quite the hatbrim-shaded leather-chapped cowgirl cometing against the stone sky of Wall Mountain, any more. No leg-swatting sagebrush grows at this altitude, and the best that she could find for headgear to herd in is Charlie's winter cap. But in wanting to be herself on horseback; in the neighborhood of high eye-opening earth; in June dreamscape of her own; in the solitary essentials of her outline today, she is enough like that picture of girl-turning-woman again.

Dreams give us lift, she's known that ever since Moss Agate. The trick is to bear up after the weight of life comes back.

Slamjam it all into herself at once and what an avalanche everybody's circumstances make. Her father in his coughing old age, ancient choreboy stuck in an annex to a chickenhouse. Wouldn't think a life could go downhill much from Moss Agate, but his has. Her mother, tough as a grindstone against her father and yet putting up with all the allowances asked by the Norskie. And her mother and Charlie, scarcely able to be civil to each other. Berneta knows too well she is at the heart of that situation, daughter-wife tug of war, but can't see much of anything to be done about. Charlie Doig and Bessie Ringer neither one is ever going to be quick to give in, and a person had better charge it off as one more price of family. You can pick your clothes/you can pick a rose/ but kin and nose/you can't pick those. Includes brothers, who're somehow both easier and harder than parents. Paul, closest to her in age and outlook, but a distancer and being made more so by the war; there in the army in Australia, he has married a Queensland nurse and gives every indication he may stay on there after the war. Wally, out on the *Ault*. She thinks his is the unfairest story, in a way. The one of all the fate-begrudged Ringers who has his essentials intact, youth and health and a warmth toward life's possibilities. Instead of the duty of war, he could be devising a life with Winona. Even when he isn't in battle it must be hard, penned up with so many people. How she'd hated that herself at Alzona Park. Aboard ship must be a double confinement. Wally lately wrote that he wonders sometimes if he is really informed about how things are with the family, whether hard news of the never-easy state of the Ringers is kept from him. Not knowing can be worse than knowing, Berneta has always savvied that too, and so she has written back a line which came out odd yet is in the pointblank attitude he seems to need from somebody on the home-front. *Don't worry, Wally—if there is anything very bad happens here at home, I'll write and tell you.*

A few lines once again to let you know that I am fine, my grandmother meanwhile works away at her weekly letter to him from her Norskie kitchen captivity. *And I hope these find you the same, Wallace.*

Her third-grade penmanship toils for whatever can be reported. Another hard rain slowing up the plowing but helping the hay. A fire in a neighbor's chickenhouse. The chance of maybe going into town to a rodeo on the Fourth of July.

Then, amid her account of rhubarb canning and doing a big load of wash, suddenly here is Winona being written off. *She's a nice enough kid in a way. But I learned Winona's ways what little time I spent with her. I nearly got my head bit off several times over nothing. It kind of amuses me about these silly girls.*

Wally's breakup loyally ratified, my grandmother makes the usual turn toward closing. *Well, dear, there doesn't seem to be much of any thing more to write about . . .*

She determinedly says nothing, yet, about Berneta out there farther than ever in the Sixteen country.

"Sixteen Creek. Sixteen Creek." The barber contemplates with his comb still trying to find some natural order to my hair. "Never been up into that country. Can a man catch a fish there if he holds his mouth right?"

"Oh-it's-so-so; the-water's-pretty-riley; ye've-got-to-fight-brush," my father guards the stream which is all but tossing trout into our frying pan.

The scissors are starting to operate around my ears. "Hold still, Sunny Jim," the barber warns me. To my father again: "Suppose we about have this war won? What do you think of this man Truman?"

Affairs of world and nation get pronounced on while I goggle out the barbershop window at all-business Bozeman. Women and more women beeline into the shops and stores. An occasional calcified male goes creaking past to a bar. Cars have the street in frequent but not frantic use. This is neither martial Phoenix nor wind-worn White Sulphur Springs, this is a sound-as-a-dollar little city catering to its plump valley.

Here comes the part of barbering I really hate, the hair tonic. This of course is a barber who likes to slosh on the pooh-pooh water, positively dousing a person's scalp with the smelly stuff and rubbing it in like analgesic. Gabbing a mile a minute while his fingers mess around up there: "This'll fix you up for the Fourth of July, got your firecrackers picked out yet?"

Now it's my father's turn under the scissors. You have to look at him twice to figure out that he only slimly has the majority of a head of hair left. The sides from the temples back are perfectly full, and the stand of hair in the middle of his head is still holding strong; it is either side of the middle that has thinned away, widow's peaks that kept on going. He has had his glasses on for reading the Bozeman paper, and looks abruptly younger again with them off.

"Always have to have the noon news," the barber announces, and turns on the radio.

Broadcasting the sheep, Berneta's patient activity now is called, in the original sense of the word. Casting them broad across the range, in a scatter so that there is maximum grass for each.

"So far so good, Flopper," she says aside to her dog partner.

Their morning pandemonium forgotten, the ewes and their copying lambs have drifted comfortably up the mountain nearly to timberline; this far up, stray jackpines stand dark against the otherwise open slope, drifters from the belt of timber. A slow-motion gamble, letting the band scatter from-hell-to-breakfast this way, but the best kind of herding if you can manage to do it. Doesn't take much tickle of the imagination to see the lambs putting on pounds as they nibble along. Keeps the herder and horse busy, though, riding a community loop around the wide-spread band to watch against all the things that sheep can get into and that can get into them. Even prettiness serves as a poison to sheep, the standing white blossoms which Berneta charges into atop Duffy and *hyaahs* a bunch of lambs away from. Fight them away from death camas in spring bloom, and away from lupine when it forms peas in autumn, you have to.

As broadcaster of sheep her mind is free to go while the rest of her has to ride the horse, and she dreams ahead now. Wouldn't know it to look at her this instant, but she is tired of being portable. She and Charlie have talked things through, the evenings in the cabin when dusk lasts in the air for hours, and reached their decision against contracting hay this summer. Stay here at the Rung place instead, is the impulse they both have. Take on the herding themselves once shearing is out of the way, using the cabin as their camp. Charlie could stand a slow summer of mending his health some more and, truth is, so could she. She can't account for it, how much better she feels in mountain circumstances, but that's the physical how of it. Not easy traveling, this rifleshot country, but you can't beat it for grass, scenery, verve of the mountain air. The rest of June and July and August here, on their own, will be a rhythm she and Charlie have not had since Grass Mountain. Even the Maudlow road can't stay muddy all summer.

Beyond, though. After August when the sheep deal is over, she and Charlie are going to have to quit thinking in seasons. Settle down and stay settled a good long while. *With Ivan starting school we are going to have to stay in one place*, Wally has been confided in, the wish told to him more than once lately. *Some place of our own.*

Time of her own, how different that'll be, too. Ivan
out of her midday hours. She enjoys a sardonic moment
thinking of that transfer, like handing along a clock that
boings whenever it feels like doing so. Going to be a
handful for the first-grade teacher, he is. Try to start him
out on *c-a-t* and first thing he'll show her he can read
catalog and everything in it. There are times she has
wondered whether it was such a smart idea to further
him in the reading as she tirelessly did, there in the
winter and night of Faulkner Creek and since; he's quite
enough of a little old man, growing up around adults all
the time instead of other children, and having his nose
in a book all the time will make him more so. But she
herself never could wait, could she, to quit being a kid.
Extend yourself full slam; if she has found anything to
believe, it's that. It reached her to Charlie, lyrical wire
in the wind. It was what pushed her to the gamble of
Ivan, chancy pregnancy atop her chancy lung health. No,
the reading and the rest of it she would not change. She
can't feel regret for how any child of hers ridge-runs the
country of his head.

A deep sound suddenly announces itself at her, part
owlhoot, part airhorn. A grouse's cry. She is sure the
alarm came from a big pine just up the slope from her,
out by itself. She checks on the sheep, finds no catastrophe
in sight, and turns to the pine. Nudging Duffy slowly
toward the tree, she tries to single out the bird. Grouse
make a riddle for the eye. Camouflaged virtually to invisible, they can sit as motionless as the treelimbs themselves. Berneta reins the horse to a quiet halt as close to
the pine as she thinks she dares, and rests forward in the

saddle. It takes her several minutes to discern the blend of feather pattern against the bark.

As if dislodged by her view of it, the grouse plunges out of the tree, wings set, sailing down the mountain. Quick and far; a hundred yards, two hundred, three hundred, the breathtaking unflapping glide goes on. At last, still without the tremor of a wing, the grouse vanishes into another tree.

All as it was; mountainside of businesslike sheep, her horseback self, tin roof of the Rung cabin far below. She notices Flop straying off in inveterate curiosity and calls him in, her voice drumming back from the mountain. That air dance of echo allures her. The play of words crisscrosses in her trial shout:

"Ringling, Ringer, Rung!"

Charlie Rung teeters in the cabin doorway, a dozen summers before, drawn by a disturbance in the air. The toot of a grouse, was that?

He squints at the meadow, quiet with hay and the blossoms of his potato patch, then up the slope of Hatfield at his handful of cows, their heads already dug into the grass again.

Not sure now he heard anything, he regrets the nips of his chokecherry wine. Homebrew for lunch is not a sound idea.

He steadies himself to look around the place, sort out what wants doing next. As ever, his eye can't get past it; the stack of house lumber, no longer the fresh yellow of when he hauled it here three years ago, four? Took receipt of it straight out of the boxcar at the Maudlow depot, borrowed the Morgans' big wagon and labored the wood in load by load, damn near tipping over every time coming up that gulch. And there the pile sits, board footage for four rooms downstairs and three up, not counting attic and screen porch. Rafters and studdings and gables and shingles, the whole shebang.

The thing of it is, the house exists in Charlie Rung's mind. The only discrepancy is that it needs to be framed up and nailed together. Time he did that. He can't fully fathom how it hasn't happened already. Hadn't he done fine with the barn? And been triple careful with the walls of the cabin, so as not to wake up some clear January morning frozen stiff? But the carpentry of the house he has not quite attended to.

Middle of June, already. Haying is about to need doing, then the barn patched and mucked out for winter, then sixty bushels of potatoes to be dug and gunnysacked and stored in the root cellar for winter, and cord after cord of stovewood to be chopped for winter too, and he is no youngster any more. All at once he knows he will never budge that lumber.

Blat is in the echoes now, the sheeps' medley of a thousand calls of *baa* bouncing here to there on Hatfield Mountain as the ewes are mothering up their lambs. They're ready to shade up, and Berneta too drops down for a rest. Army of mothers, encampment of wool at the top of the mountainslope. Berneta unwraps her sandwiches for lunch and gives Flop a share.

*   *   *

Out of the barbershop Dad and I march, shining at the back of the neck, and hurry through egg salad sandwiches at the lunch counter of the drugstore. The day is going and, last bite down, so are we.

Onward to conspiracy. This is the part that is secret from Berneta. My father had confided it to me as soon as we turned Prince Al loose. I outright dance to the idea, and my father looks like he could spring down the street in a burst of jigsteps himself.

At our destination, though, two of the women shoppers who seem to be the occupying force of Bozeman are passing by, one shaking her head and telling the other: "You ought to just see the prices they've got in there."

" 'Spensive?"

"Awful. I walked in and walked out."

The Doigs are not daunted. In we plunge, my father's jaw geared forward into determination.

Shelves, counters, racks, boxes. Storeload of stuff, and the saleswoman is busy with a woman customer buying something whispery. We're on our own and glad of it.

"What's it a present for?" I'd asked my father when he unveiled this intrigue of his.

That threw him for a moment. Nearly three months yet to Berneta's birthday, and their wedding anniversary had been six, no, already seven weeks ago.

"The first day of summer," he resorted to. "Approximate."

This was good, though. My father feeling relieved

enough about the arc of the sheep deal so far, about cabin life and the summer range, to think in gift terms. Berneta has been through a lot, this hobo quintet of months since he fell sick in Alzona Park. Time for her to have a surprise of the decent sort.

My father zeroes in on the merchandise he has in mind. Picks one up and eyes it as if trying to see through it.

"What color would ye say this is, Ivan?"

How to define that it has a kind of off-reddish tint, neither quite one color nor another, stumps me until I think to declare: "Hereford."

"That's no good to us then," he puts it sharply down. "We want straight brown, so it'll go with anything."

I manage to single out undiluted brown, my father decides on the fanciest style, and we're already halfway in business. Away we swagger to another section of the store, for the other item of splurge to go with this one.

There, the saleswoman catches up with us. We feel we don't noticeably need her help, but she seems to think otherwise.

"This brown is close enough to the other one," she undertakes to show us, "to go together nicely."

"Close enough isn't what we're after," my father lets her know.

Down cascade more boxes of the item, the saleswoman displaying one after another until I exercise our proxy on the precise same color.

Dad names the size, and the saleswoman wonders if that doesn't sound too big. My father gives no ground. He knows the size of everything Berneta wears, and

barely keeps from telling the snooty salesclerk it was all
volunteer arithmetic, too.

The saleswoman wants to know what other assistance
she can render us. My father informs her the spree is
over, how much are the damages? She adds up the set of
purchases, he flips his checkbook out and writes the figure
as if it was pocket change. Away, rich in gifts, we go
again.

Groceries next, by the boxload. The trunk of the Ford
swallows it all away and my father looks twice at his
wristwatch. All we need now is Prince Al. Naturally he
has not shown up, here at the hour Dad absolutely in-
structed him to.

My father starts to stew. The thirty-five-mile drive
yet ahead, mudholes in ambush; a stop at the Morgans
to tell them we've done our own camptending this week;
tarping the groceries into slingpacks behind our saddles;
the three-mile horseback ride from the mouth of the
gulch up to the cabin—he doesn't want added into all
that a door-to-door search of Bozeman for Prince goddamn Al.

"Daddy, are you going to can him?"

"To even do that we need to find the sonofabuck." As
much to the lengthy main street of Bozeman as to himself
or me, he addresses: "Where do ye suppose a bird like
him would hang out?"

Choices are plenty, although all in one category. Just
from where we stand I can read the twinkling signs of
several nominees—the Crystal Bar, the Rocking R Bar,
the Park Bar, the Stockman Bar.

My father casts another glance, this time at the sun,

midway down the afternoon sky, and starts us toward the nearest of the bars at his racing pace. "Bastard him anyway, we don't have the time—"

Time to head down out of here, Berneta can tell from her glance at the sun; start the sheep moving down the mountain toward the place for night.

The sheep, contrary old sisters that they can be, have forgotten their earlier affection for the bedground and want to keep on stuffing grass into themselves. Words fly out over the mountain: "Around them, Flop. *Way* around them." While the dog makes his rounds, Berneta adds whistling and a clatter chorus of cans. Grudgingly, the ewes shift around and mince slowly down the slope, their lambs skittery at their sides. It will be a push, to make them move down to the cabin meadow before dark. The horse and dog both are showing themselves tired and, message from her body, she is getting seriously that way, too. Stay on the horse, she again reminds herself. Riding is work, but walking this vast sidehill is more so. She spurs Duffy closer to the herd.

"Of-all-the-goddamn-times-to-have-to-herd-the-god-damn-herder," my father tells the world. He and I ransack the drinkeries on the south side of the street first, Dad giving a description of Prince Al which grows more blazing with each bar. But the bartenders shake their heads, chorus that they sure haven't laid eyes on any such specimen. We even resort to the Oaks Cigar Store, on the chance he's in there stoking up on chaw.

No luck. "Worse mess, if we go back out without him," my father reminds himself by stating to me, and we begin canvassing the north side of the street.

Who would have thought it of scruffy gopher-cheeked Prince Al? He was ensconced in the cocktail lounge of the swanky Baxter Hotel, the absolute last place to look, pickling himself with mixed drinks called Brown Bombers.

"Got your compensation fixed up, it looks like," my father begins with mere sarcasm, then he really lights into him. Takes the hide off him for breaking his word about meeting us on time, for going off on a bender, for general misbehavior while a woman has to handle his sheep for him. Yet not quite firing him. We still desperately need a herder, even one of this candlepower, until shearing.

Without a word, Prince Al follows us out and folds himself into the car.

The route from the Maudlow road up to the cabin was beginning to take on familiar features, like a caravan run. The creek dodged through the thick brush, every ripple purring in hiding. Yellow shaley rock cliffed out wherever the gulch broke at a bend. Ahead, overhead, Hatfield Mountain topping out in its thatch of timber. At the halfway point, the sudden stand of low-branched cottonwoods to watch out for or they would slap you half off your horse.

I nod along in the dreamslow rhythm of the ride, perched, lulled, being carried by event. But go to my father and he is remaking the day, casting away the delay and lateness, churning worry into reassurance: if it would only stay churned. Holy-J.-Christ, his mood runs, how-can-ye-ever-figure-it-all? Prince Al possibly would've behaved himself, not gone off and got plastered, if Berneta had been the one to take him to town. Yet, couldn't really blame her for not wanting to fight the Maudlow road; lucky enough that my father didn't get us stuck himself, in those mudholes that would swallow a person's shadow. Besides, maybe Prince Al would've fallen off the wagon even if a dozen Bernetas had taken him to town, maybe he was just that kind. But oh damn the weather that we were always having to try to sneak past, outguess, make muddy choices. If it'll only let us settle in; the Rung place is restful when it's not a day of commotion like this. The sheep deal will pay off in just a couple more weeks, at shearing. Then there'll be the lamb money this fall, and even a bit of profit at selling the ewes too; money enough to set us up for a good long time. We can see if Berneta will try Arizona again, that ranch country around Prescott. Or if she can get by in Montana as well as she has this spring, maybe that's as much as can be asked. Ivan in school this fall, we'll need to place ourselves and we will. Not far now to the cabin. Damn-it-all-to-hell-anyway, how late in the day it's gotten to be. But her stint with the sheep ought to have gone well, browsing them a little way up the mountain like he had laid out for her. And the weather hadn't been terrible, which qualified it as good. And she is veteran at all this, after all. Knows the country, Berneta does. Knows herself, better even than he's ever managed to. What was it she'd said? "Don't worry none, I'm not about to walk myself to—"

*   *   *

Dearth of activity at the meadow, the cabin, as we file up out of the tangly gulch.

It is nearing dark. The sheep are bedded at the upper end of the meadow, where my father had conveniently sited the herder's tepee that morning. Prince Al, sobering up grumpy, heads his horse toward the tepee.

Duffy, still saddled, is grazing in the high grass alongside the barn. Berneta is nowhere in sight.

My father stands in his stirrups, suddenly tiptoe with the strain of trying to see behind the cabin windows slurred with dusk. "Berneta, we're home," he shouts almost as if it were a question.

The cabin.

The barn.

The bedded sheep.

Nothing answers him except echo.

Then in the frame of the cabin doorway, just distinct. Wiping her hands with a sack towel, she calls out:

"Back the same day, are you."

The sheepdogs appear, one on either side of her, yawning from their cozy cabin stay.

Burden of worry off him now, my father clucks his horse into faster pace across the meadow. I bounce on the back of Star, trying to keep up.

They've all kissed and gone on to generalities about the day by the time I slide down from my horse. My mother hugs me and calls me her Boze*man Ivan*, laughs that Dad and I don't seem to be cut out for town barbering, we've come home looking like a couple of scared preachers.

My father does a necessary asking. "How'd ye do with the sheep?"

Her day on the mountain revolves again. The sheep when they were pigheaded, the sheep when they were perfect. Varieties of weather. Taste of the sandwich lunch, sound of the grouse. Exasperation, exaltation, sufficiency of each. Common day in the week of life.

She sums it as she will for Wally, in transoceanic ink, in the morning:

I got along okay.

The mail and groceries have to wait. First out of the pack are the conspiratorial boxes for her. This, my father the cowboy suitor could perform blind. "We happened to bring ye a couple little somethings, dear," he pronounces and flourishes the first box to her, then with a grin hands me the other one to hand to her.

"What have you two been up to?" She gazes, as captured with surprise as we could wish, back and forth at my identically grinning father and me.

"Try 'em on," my father says with acey-deucey confidence.

Publicly done, as everything is in the single room of the cabin. She slips the first item on, exclaims to us about the perfect fit, which of course we knew. She peeks in the second box.

Lifts out the other half of the outfit with an "Oh, I ought to send you two to town all the time." Puts it on by ducking down to adjust it just-so in Dad's shaving mirror.

Turns to us, rigged out new from head to toe.
*Charlie and Ivan brought me the nicest pair of brown
boots and a big hat.*
So I am a combination cowgirl sheepherder now.

Away to the *Ault* flowed that third June letter of hers,
full of her herding triumph and the summer to be ridden
into with newly given garb. Somewhere it crossed mail-
paths with the only letter from Wally that has come to
light.

All his others, nearly a steady year's worth from such
war addresses as Pearl Harbor and Iwo Jima and Eni-
wetok and Luzon and Okinawa, went the way of discard
and loss. But this single one hid in plain sight, in print.
Proudly sent to the editor of the White Sulphur Springs
weekly newspaper by my grandmother, it appears in full
on the front page of July 4, 1945. *Now don't think that
this is all that could be said,* Wally tags on an immediate
warning. *It is what they will let past the censors.*

*. . . Many exciting encounters . . . helping to make his-
tory each day . . . bringing the end of the war nearer . . .*
Beyond the dehydrated handout to send to the folks at
home, the *Ault* was wending its own route through the
last of the Pacific war. The ship is in Samuel Eliot Mori-
son's naval history of World War Two, a photograph of
the destroyer taking on fuel in heavy seas, white water
smashing over its every deck. The *Ault* and Wally ultimately would make it into Tokyo Bay for the ceremony
of surrender by Japan. A night soon after, something
Wally and the other young sailors had never seen: their

ship's running lights. (Logbook of the *Ault*: BY ORDER
OF COMMANDER TASK GROUP, ALL SHIPS TURNED ON
NAVIGATIONAL LIGHTS FOR THE FIRST TIME SINCE DE-
CEMBER 7, 1941.) Three hundred forty-five men co-
cooned in a skinny vessel three hundred sixty-nine feet
long, the *Ault* crew survived to do its own telling of the
war.

Don't think that this is all that could be said. What was
slighted worst of all in the officially prepared letter home
for Wally and the other *Ault* men was the actual business
of war, taking toll. Nowhere the sense that this promised
to be the to-the-death summer when an American bomber
sent down a new manner of bomb which torched the city
of Hiroshima in white-hot radiation, and then repeated
on the city of Nagasaki. Deliberate amnesia of hurt and
death is the order of the day. The *Ault*'s sailors had
watched planes burst into fireballs over them, had
plucked survivors and bodies from the ocean when the
carriers *Wasp* and *Franklin* and *Hancock* and *Bunker Hill*
were aflame, had felt the close pass of kamikaze attacks,
had fed ammunition into hypnotic gunchambers through
eighty straight days of Okinawa combat. But the official
warworld of Wally's ship is rounded off to: *We have our
less happy times . . .*

Only the letter's closing lines seem not canned, start
to sound like true Wally again. The Wally who can't
bring himself to stay listless even in censored circumstances. *Some of it is not as bad as it sounds*, the feel of his
war comes out on paper, *Some of it was worse.* He leaves
off in a dreamtime of his own, sailor Montanan trying
to deploy himself into a future. *This is just about our last*

operation. . . . Maybe next spring we will get to see each other again.

In the column exactly beside Wally's letter was printed my mother's obituary.

Word came aboard the *Ault* in the worst possible way, in a p.s. miserably penciled onto one of my grandmother's weekly letters to Wally.

Dear Wallace, some awful sad news to tell you since I wrote your letter. Berneta passed away last nite. That's all the word I've gotten so far. I don't know where they're at or where she died at.

She didn't suffer any at the last, Wally—the pencilscript now my father's shaken hand in an ensuing letter—*for which I am thankful. She was feeling extra good all evening and we talked until eleven that night. She passed away at 2:30 A.M. on the 27th of June, Ivan's birthday. I didn't even have time to awaken Ivan, she went so fast.*

Swift, then, the attack by which she died. Not the customary siege of short breath, the jolting coughs and lung convulsions, the air-short fatigue, that she had ridden out so many times before. Not the open mayhem of asthma. Instead on her death certificate, *immediate cause* is given as an overstretching of the cardiac muscle—which was to say, a heart condition. Nowhere ever written, then or since, was the simultaneous fact of earth: the acrobat heights of Montana earth that kept her so alive, until they killed her.

*   *   *

Nobody got over her. Doig or Ringer, those around me in my growing-up stayed hit, pierced, by my mother's death in the mountain cabin.

My father was wrenched back and forth by how welcome the return to Montana had been for Berneta, and how treacherously it struck her down; how risky the one last mountain summer turned out to be, how unsaveable his wife's health ultimately was.

To my grandmother, her suspicion of "out there" was horridly proven, Berneta taken from her in some remote visitless place. Having had to toughen herself against so much, Bessie Ringer now faced what would never go away, death of a daughter.

For Wally, the reaction was a lifelong clutch at his sister's last letters, the keeping of news which shot in just when it had become clear that he himself would survive the war.

Always after, for all of us, it was not simply that Berneta had died young. There was always the echo-plus of "out there in the Sixteen country," "up there on the mountain," "on Ivan's sixth birthday." A private family dialect of magnitude and conjunction and consequence. The Sixteen country held that magnified proportion for my mother; her manner of death held it for those who most loved her.

On through that summer of 1945, the last of the letters in Wally's packet were written and sent out in misery and confusion, several by my grandmother and a pair by my father.

Brittle and cracking a bit more each time I unfold them, they still manage to stab. *So blue*, my grandmother lets down onto the page, *seems all I do is cry & cry some more.* My father tries to convey the deadweight of time on him now. *No one can understand it that hasn't been through it. The days are weeks and the weeks are months for me.* Then, sad dream going into nightmare, their lines turn and spit sour toward each other.

I haven't seen your mother for a long time, Wally.

Wallace dearest, I haven't seen Charlie or Ivan since we laid Berneta away.

She never comes around to see Ivan.

I've got no way to go see them. Then I haven't the heart to go where Charlie is anyway.

She could have come nearer giving Ivan mother love than any other person in the world.

Got a letter from Charlie yesterday in answer to the one I wrote and asked him if I could help them in any way. But he gave me to understand that I wasn't fit to help take care of Ivan. The only way he can think of me is with pity and regret.

I feel bad to think she and I can't get along.

He knows he can hurt me through Ivan.

I shall try so hard to bring Ivan up to be the kind of son his mother would wish.

I'll write Ivan but I'll not write him.

It took my father and my grandmother five more years to quit their grievous scrap, but that was a lot better than never.

In the last twist of all, they turned together to raise me. When my father faced himself in the glass door of a phone booth in White Sulphur Springs a night in 1950 and went through with the long-distance call to the Norskie country, he closed down the war that had begun over Berneta and continued over Berneta's child. As my grandmother managed to swallow away as much grudge as she heard being swallowed at the other end of the line, she volunteered herself yet another time into a shortsided situation, never to be a wife nor even a lover, not the mother of me yet something beyond grandparent. From then on, the cook during haying or calving or lambing at the ranches where my father worked was Bessie instead of Berneta, the couple who would throw themselves and their muscles into sheep deals were Charlie and his

154

mother-in-law instead of his young wife. I grew up amid their storms, for neither of these two was ever going to know the meaning of pallid. But as their truce swung and swayed and held, my growing-up felt not motherless but tribal, keenly dimensional, full of alliances untranslatable but ultimately gallant (*no, she's not my mother, she's . . . no, he's my father, not my grand-*) and loyalties deep as they were complex. So many chambers, of those two and of myself, I otherwise would have never known.

In the eventual, when I had grown and gone, my grandmother and father stayed together to see each other on through life. April 6, 1971: his time came first, from emphysema which was the cruel lung reprise of my mother's fate. October 24, 1974: my grandmother remained sturdy to her final instant—one mercy at last on these people, her death moment occurred in the middle of a chuckle as she joked with a friend driving her to a card party at the Senior Citizens Club.

Their twenty-one years together, a surprising second life for each, I've long known I was the beneficiary of. The letters teach me anew, though, how desperately far they had to cross from that summer of grief. Theirs was maybe the most durable dreaming of all, that not-easy pair; my father and my grandmother, and their boundaryless memory of my mother.

And I see at last, past the curtain of time which fell prematurely between us, that I am another one for whom my mother's existence did not end when her life happened to.

Summoning myself—summing myself—is no less

complicated, past fifty, than it was in the young-eyed blur at those howling Montana gravesides. *Doig, Ivan, writer: independent as a mule, bleeder for the West's lost chances, exile in the Montana diaspora from the land, second-generation practical thrower of flings, emotionally skittish of opening himself up like a suitcase, delver into details to the point of pedantry, dreamweaver on a professional basis*—some of me is indisputably my father and my grandmother, and some I picked up along the way. But another main side of myself, I recognize with wonder in the reflection of my mother's letters. It turns out that the chosen world where I strive to live full slam—earth of alphabet, the Twenty-Six country—had this earlier family inhabitant who wordworked, played seriously at phrase, cast a sly eye at the human herd; said onto paper her loves and her fears and her endurance in between; most of all, from somewhere drew up out of herself the half hunch, half habit—the have-to—of eternally keeping score on life, trying to coax out its patterns in regular report, making her words persevere for her. Berneta Augusta Maggie Ringer Doig, as distinct as the clashes of her name.

Ivan is fine, growing like a weed, her pen closes off its last letter ever, June 19, 1945. *You don't need to worry about him forgetting you, he remembers his Uncle Wally and knows what ship you are on. He'll probably have a million questions to ask when you get back.*

A million minus one, now. The lettered answer of origins, of who first began on our family oceans of asking. As I put words to pages, I voyage on her ink.

ACKNOWLEDGMENTS

Carol Doig for her keen eye as a research photographer and manuscript reader, and her customary love and reliability; Dave and Marcella Walter for their knowledge of Montana and its history, and the loan of their four-wheel-drive rig for revisiting the Maudlow country; the late Anna Doig Beetem for details about Alzona Park; the Phoenix Public Library, the Arizona Historical Society, the Arizona Historical Foundation, the libraries of the University of Arizona and Arizona State University, and the Montana Historical Society for backdrop material about Arizona and Montana during World War Two; the Desert Caballeros Western Museum in Wickenburg for information and photos dealing with that community in 1945, and Linda Brown and Rosemary Clark at the Wickenburg Public Library for guiding me through the *Wickenburg Sun* files and other holdings; Elinore S. Thomas of the Corporate Communications Department of the Aluminum Company of America for information about the Phoenix defense plant workforce; Tab Lewis of the Civil Reference Branch of the National Archives for the Defense Plant Corporation floor plan and inventory of the Phoenix plant; Deborah Nash and Nathan Bender of the Merrill G. Burlingame Special Collections at the library of Montana State University, for details of Bozeman in 1945; "Winona" and her husband for their hospitality and talk of the past; the Naval Historical Center, and particularly Bernard F. Cavalcante, head of the Operational Archives Branch, for the action reports and war diary of the destroyer USS *Ault*; the National Archives for photocopies of the *Ault*'s logbook from Dec. 1, 1944 to Sept. 30, 1945 and for the homestead file of Charlie Rung; David Palmer of Flinders University of South Australia, for the Kearny Shipyard specifications of the *Ault*; Marshall J. Nelson for being Marshall J. Nelson; R. L. Prescott for his memories of Allen and Winnie Prescott; the late Paul Ringer of Rockhampton, Queensland, for his reflective correspondence with me on the family feud between my father and my grandmother; Theresa Buckingham for her recollections of my mother and father, and for her insight on the way my father wore his hat cocked; Linda Bierds for being my volunteer muse on yet another manuscript; Joyce Justice of the Federal Records Center in Seattle, for steering me toward the relevant holdings in the National Archives; the late John Gruar for his recollection of my mother's trapline; Zoe Kharpertian for her deft blue pencil; Liz Darhansoff and Lee Goerner for their usual valuable ministrations in the book biz—*Heart Earth* and I are grateful to them all.

As is told in this book, Berneta Doig's letters from February to June of 1945 were left to me upon the death of my uncle, Wally Ringer, and I want to particularly thank my cousins, Dan Ringer and Dave Ringer, for searching out and providing me the packet of letters their father wanted me to have. A word about my quotations from the letters herein: I am a writer, not a transcriber, and so when I felt it necessary for clarity of the storyline, I have shifted sentences into an earlier scene than their actual postmark, have taken out an occasional cumbersome bit such as "kind of," and standardized my mother's references to *her* mother as both "Mom" and "Mama" to simply "Mom," to try to lessen confusion. And for the miner's soliloquy on the wagon traffic jam in Deadwood, I have drawn on an early "oral history" interview of freight wagon driver Clarence Palmer, as provided me by the late Vernon Carstensen. As to the German POWs, the frequency of their escapes was even greater than my parents suspected; Arnold P. Krammer in "German Prisoners of War in the United States," *Military Affairs*, April 1976, points out that "the average monthly escape rate from June 1944 to August 1945 . . . was over 100, or an average of 3 to 4 escapes per day." My reference to the "mortal evaporation" that Montana suffered in World War Two is based on the facts that Montanans, in proportion to population, served in the armed forces in numbers higher than the national average, and that Montana's war dead, again proportionally, was exceeded only by New Mexico's among the then-forty-eight states. (Montana also had been hard hit by World War One, when the state's incorrectly high draft call and high voluntarism combined to inflict the highest toll of war dead, proportionally, of all the states.) The specific theaters of combat in which residents of our area, Meagher County, served were compiled from issues of the weekly *Meagher County News*; my uncle's letter from the Pacific and my mother's obituary are both in the July 4, 1945 issue of that newspaper. And finally, the concept of the "Western Civil War of Incorporation," for which I am indebted to the historian Richard Maxwell Brown, his book *No*

Duty to Retreat (New York: Oxford University Press, 1991), and its defining insight that "in the West the incorporation trend resulted in what should at last be recognized as a civil war across the entire expanse of the West—one fought in many places and on many fronts in almost all the Western territories and states from the 1860s and beyond."

ABOUT THE AUTHOR

Acclaim for Ivan Doig's work began with his 1978 book, *This House of Sky*, a finalist for the National Book Award in contemporary thought. "The language begins in western territory and experience but in the hands of an artist it touches all landscape and all life," wrote Robert Kirsch in the *Los Angeles Times*. "Doig is such an artist." His books since then have been the non-fiction *Winter Brothers* and the novels *The Sea Runners*, *English Creek*, *Dancing at the Rascal Fair* and *Ride with Me, Mariah Montana*. Born in the Montana mountain country he writes of in *Heart Earth*, Mr. Doig has worked as a ranch hand, newspaperman, magazine editor and writer. In 1989 the Western Literature Association honored him with its Distinguished Achievement Award for his body of work. He lives in Seattle with his wife, Carol, who teaches the Literature of the American West.